MARILYN · THE ULTIMATE LOOK AT THE LEGEND

MARILYN
THE ULTIMATE LOOK AT THE LEGEND

JAMES HASPIEL

HENRY HOLT AND COMPANY

NEW YORK

It is with profound respect and love that
this work, which has taken thirty-nine years of my
existence to bring to life, is dedicated to . . .

JAMES FITZGERALD SMITH

Thank you for bringing me back into the light.

Henry Holt and Company, Inc.
Publishers since 1866
115 West 18th Street
New York, New York 10011

Henry Holt ® is a registered trademark of
Henry Holt and Company, Inc.

Library of Congress Cataloging-in-Publication Data

Haspiel, James.
   [Marilyn]
  Marilyn: The ultimate look at the legend / James Haspiel—
1st American ed.
     p.   cm.
    Originally published in Great Britain as: Marilyn:
the ultimate look at the legend.
    1. Monroe, Marilyn, 1926–1962.   2. Motion
picture actors and actresses—United States—
Biography.   I. Title.
PN2287.M69H35   1991
791.43′028′092—dc20
[B]

91-17365
CIP

ISBN 0–8050–1856–5
ISBN 0–8050–2965–6 (An Owl Book: pbk.)

Henry Holt books are available for special promotions
and premiums. For details contact:
Director, Special Markets.

First published in Great Britain in 1991 by
Smith Gryphon Publishers.
First published in the United States in 1991 by
Henry Holt and Company, Inc.

First Owl Book edition—1993

Designed by Hammond Hammond

Printed in Italy by New Interlitho SpA
All first editions are printed on acid-free paper. ∞

10 9 8 7 6 5 4 3 2 1
10 9 8 7 6 5 4 3 2 1 (pbk.)

CONTENTS

BEFORE MARILYN

Norma Jeane arrived at the orphanage, the institution the Mortenson girl would now call home, at age nine. Sitting on the end of her cot, she peered intensely out of a window facing the water tower resting atop the RKO movie studio located nearby. Norma Jeane's mother had worked at that studio as a film cutter, shortly before she had become too ill to deal with life in the outside world and was taken away to a mental institution. Gladys Mortenson was to remain there for decades to come. What the young girl did not know was that one day, she too would work at the RKO studio, stepping onto a soundstage there to go before their motion picture cameras as an actress in a film to be called *Clash by Night*.

For the child, Norma Jeane, it had all begun on June 1st, 1926. When the doctor slapped her tiny behind at nine-thirty that morning, the action was the onset of an endless amount of abuse destined to come her way, out of which she herself would rise up engulfed in an essence of purity and luminescence not easily equalled in this world before or since.

Norma Jeane's first memory was to be a profoundly prophetic one, the terrifying moment when her mother's mother attempted to snuff out her infant life: 'I can still remember waking up from my afternoon nap fighting for my life. She had something pressed against my face, a pillow, and I fought with all my strength till it stopped.' Now, both her grandmother and her mother were beyond hurting her again, at least physically.

As the next years telescoped by, Norma Jeane would depart the orphanage to live with a variety of foster families. It is certainly improbable that Norma Jeane Mortenson ever knew about an obituary printed in the *New York Times* newspaper of November 5th,

This early studio portrait of Marilyn, taken in 1953, evokes the image of an earlier Hollywood sex-symbol, Jean Harlow.

GIRL DIES AT GAME

Miss Monroe of East Orange Is Stricken at Williams Field

Special to THE NEW YORK TIMES.

WILLIAMSTOWN, Mass., Nov. 4 —Miss Marilyn Monroe, 17 years old, of East Orange, N. J., died here this afternoon.

Her brother, Malcolm Monroe, a junior at Williams, had escorted her to the Williams-Union football game on Weston Field.

When she became ill she was taken to the Hallern Inn, where Drs. Coughlin, MacCready, Farnsworth and Locke attended her. She died shortly after 5 P. M.

Dr. Locke, director of health and athletics at Williams, said that Miss Monroe had been stricken "presumably by a cerebral hemorrhage."

New York Times 11-5-39

1939, reporting the unfortunate demise of a seventeen-year-old girl named, would you believe, Marilyn Monroe; the very name with which Norma Jeane was to make cinema history.

At sixteen, Norma Jeane wed. She was to write loving letters about her husband, 'Jimmie', before their subsequent problems and divorce in 1946. By this time, she was becoming a professional model, soon to be a fully nude calendar girl. In all, the events of her still young life until now would be but a prelude to her entry into a profession that would ultimately render her an authentic legend, Norma Jeane's eventual emergence into the incredible world of acting in motion pictures.

'I never wanted her to go into that business!' The voice being directed at me in 1972 belonged to the architect of Norma Jeane's very being, her mother, Gladys. The meeting was, for me, a compelling one. We spoke about her daughter for nearly two hours. As I took my leave of Gladys, her firm words about Norma Jeane echoed in my ears: 'I never wanted her . . .'

'Marilyn Monroe' stared back at me in 1969, these words printed on the face of her burial crypt. Yes, she was now in there behind the marble slab. But in there, too, were the remains of Marilyn Miller (her name by her marriage to the great American playwright, Arthur Miller), Marilyn DiMaggio (by her marriage to the American baseball legend, Joe DiMaggio), Jean Norman (a name she had used on a magazine cover, while still a model), Norma Jeane Dougherty (her name by her marriage to 'Jimmie'), and, of course, the real occupant of the space I now stood before, Norma Jeane Mortenson. All of them were now finally at rest. For sure, she had had an incredible life, and fate had dictated that her life intermingle with mine for one long and magical moment – ergo, this personal memoir.

THE BIRTH OF NORMA JEANE

Above: Marilyn's birth certificate shows the spelling she used for her name on all personal correspondence and formal documents – Norma Jeane with the final 'e'.

Left above: The General Hospital building in Los Angeles where Norma Jeane was born on the morning of June 1st, 1926.

Left below: Hollygrove orphanage which Norma Jeane saw for the first time at the age of nine, after her mother was finally committed to an institution.

Marilyn's mother, Gladys Mortenson. I met her in 1972, after another writer had claimed she was dead. She was a passionate Christian Scientist, who at first was reluctant to talk about her daughter.

MARRIAGE TO JIM DOUGHERTY

Miss Ana Lower
requests the honour of your presence
at the marriage of her niece
Norma Jean Baker
to
Mr. James E. Dougherty
Friday, the nineteenth of June
nineteen hundred and forty-two
at 8:30 o'clock p. m.
at the home of
Mr. and Mrs. Chester Howell
432 South Bentley Avenue
Los Angeles, California

Reception
Immediately after ceremony
432 South Bentley Avenue
Los Angeles, California

Above and opposite: Norma Jeane weds 'Jimmie' Dougherty. Although during the Second World War he was often away from home, Norma Jeane was, for most of her marriage, happy with her first husband.

Above: Her first wedding invitation, issued by her 'aunt', Ana Lower, on which the final 'e' was mistakenly omitted from Norma Jeane's name.

Overleaf: The fond letters to her guardian, Grace Goddard, show the enormous love Norma Jeane had for Jimmie.

"DEAREST GRACE . . . ."

~~Three Delthia~~ St.
~~Van Nuys~~, California
June 15, 1944.

Dearest Grace,

I was so happy to hear from you. I was so thrilled to read you letter and learn of all that you have been doing lately.

I will send you your picture very sortly now, I'm going down saturday to find out more about it. Also will send you lots of snap shots at the same time I send you the picture. I found out that a 10" x 12" (that was the size you wanted wasn't it?) cost exactly $5.00.

Jimmie has been gone for seven weeks and the first word I ~~received~~ received ~~from him~~ was the day before my birthday. He sent a

Cable Night Letter by Western Union saying "Darling, on your birth day, I send you a whole world of Love". I was simply thrilled to death to hear from him.

I have never really written and told you of Jimmies and me married life together. Of course I know that if it hadn't been for you we might not have ever been married and I know I owe you a lot for that fact alone, besides countless others. That is why I feel that I should let you know about us. I love Jimmie just more than anyone (in a different way I suppose than anyone) and I know I shall never be happy with anyone else as long

as I live, and I know he feels ~~that~~ the same towards me. So you see we are really very happy together that is of course, when we can be together. We both miss each other terribly. We will be married two years June 19th. And we really have had quite a happy life to-gether.

I am working 10 hrs. a day at Radio plane Co., at Metropolitain airport. I am saving almost everything I earn (to help pay for our future home after the war) The work isn't easy at all for I am on my feet all day and walking quite a bit.

I was all set to get a Civil Service Job with the Army, all my

papers filled out and every thing set to go, and then I found out I would be working with all ~~military~~ army fellows. I was over there one day, There are just too many wolves to be working with, there are enough of those at Radio plane Co. with out a whole army full of them. The Personal Officer said that he would hire me but that he wouldn't advice it for my own sake, so I am back at Radio plane Co. pretty contented.

Well I guess that is about all for now.

With much love,
Norma Jeane

Sunday December 3, 1944

Dearest Grace,

Thank you so much for the little black dress you sent to me, I just love it. All it will need is just shortening and taken in around the wasit and hips. It was awfully sweet of you to send it to me.

As much as I like that black dress (with the pink satin) I just couldn't keep it, Grace, because

2

it just fits you and it looks so nice on you. I would have to have it fixed and besides I just wouldn't feel right about it, its such an expensive dress and all, though it was so sweet of you to want to give it to me. I shall just borrow it as I am doing with the hat.

I found out that its possible to buy a Gold Coast Monkey Coat. I shall write to you about it later.

3—

I had very enjoyable trip from Chicago to Los Angeles, I wasn't sick even once. Every one was just grand to me on the train, I'll tell you all about it sometime.

Jimmie hasn't come home yet, maybe he might make it before Christmas, but he doesn't think so. I certainly hope he'll be home, it just won't seem right without him, I love him so very much, honestly I don't think there is another man alive like him. He really is awfully sweet.

4—

I hope your not working so hard now Grace, and getting more rest and sleep. Please write to me about your self.

I shall send you more money a little later.

I can't ever tell you how much the trip did for me, I shall be forever greatfull to you Grace. I love you and Daddy so much. I sure miss you Grace.

With Love,
XOXOXOXO   Norma Jeane
P.S. tell everyone at the Studio "hello".

June 4th/1945.

My Dearest Grace,

I'm awfully sorry I haven't written sooner but honestly I have been so busy trying to get moved, getting Jimmie ready to leave and just a million things at one time.

I haven't worked at Radioplane Company since January. They keep asking me to come back but

I don't really want to do that kind of work any more because it makes me so darn tired, I just don't care about anything when I'm that tired.

The day I went back to work, after my trip back East with you, they had some Army photographers there at work and they were taking Moving Pictures for Army training.

The first thing I knew the leadlady and leadman had me out there having the Army taking Pictures of me. They all asked where in the H--- I had been hiding. I told them I had been back east on leave of absence, with my folks.

They took a lot of moving pictures of me, and some of them asked for dates etc. (Naturally I refused!)

They were all nice Army officers and men. After they finished with some of the pictures. A Army Cpl. by the name of David Conover told me he would be very interested in getting some color still shots of me. He use to have a studio on "the strip" on sunset. He said he would make arrangements with the Plant superintendent if I would agree so I said okay he told me what to wear and

what shade lipstick etc.
so the next couple of
weeks I posed for
him at differn't times,
when ever he could
get over to the plant.
He had to come from
Culver City each time. He
is now with the 1st Motion
Picture Unit.
He called me at the
plant one morning later
and said that all the
pictures came out perfect
Also he said that I

should by all means
go into Modeling prof.
He also said that I
phographed very well
and that he wants to
take a lot more. Also he
said he had a lot of
contacts in which he wanted
me to look into.
I told him I would
rather not work when
Jimmie was here so he
said he would wait, so
I'm expecting to hear

from him most any time
again. He called not
Long ago and said he
had a lot more prints
for me to keep.
He is awfully nice and
is married and is strictly
business, which is the
way I like it. Jimmy
seems to like the Idea
of me modeling so I'm
glad about that.
I'm going to ask David
Conover for some more
prints and I'll send you

some
what do you hear from
Ray Wolfe? Do you
still think that Daddy can
fix it up okay?
I shall be so happy
to see you again dear
and to see Daddy and
Bebe, because I love
you all so much.
I'll write again tomorrow,
I promise!

With Love,
Norma Jean.
XOXOXOXO

P.S. Please excuse me writing
because I'm in a hurry.

COVER GIRL

Right: This first cover, in 1946, was far removed from the future sex symbol image of Marilyn Monroe.

NORMA JEAN DOUGHERTY

Opposite: During the mid-1940s, she was the cover girl on numerous magazines. There is, incidentally, an interesting 'Jean Norman' credit in the bottom left corner of this collection.

Right: Norma Jeane's application to the Blue Book Model Agency. A chance meeting with army photographer, David Conover, at the Radioplane Company in California, and described by Marilyn in the letter on the previous pages, led her to the Agency and to making this film test shot (*above*). She preferred to drop the final 'e' from Jeane in her professional credits at this time.

ENTER MARILYN MONROE

=DAILY= VARIETY =DAILY=

Thur., Sept. 5, 1946

HALF BILLION IN
FILM TILL FOR
...IN

...age 1 ♥

...wo, financial
...evelopment,
...by the tre-
...ing capital
...y over the

...erlying the
...l cash de-

...roduction

...cations of

...markets.
...tre part-
...court de-

...der new

...lid fin-
...more
...result
...he war

...stry's
...1940-
...e un-
...,000

...to the
...ze of
...figure
...k of
...tion
...on

...he
...at
...w

...t
...–
...ot

20th CENTURY-FOX

Twentieth Century-Fox Film Corporation

STUDIOS
BEVERLY HILLS, CALIFORNIA

February 10, 1947

Miss Marilyn Monroe)
(Norma Jeane Dougherty)
c/o National Concert & Artists Corporation
9059 Sunset Blvd.
Los Angeles 46, California

Dear Miss Monroe:

This letter, when accepted by you, will confirm our mutual understanding and agreement relative to the amendment of your contract of employment with us, dated August 24, 1946, as follows, but not otherwise:

It is mutually understood and agreed that we do hereby exercise the option granted to us by the terms of your said contract of employment with us to extend the term of the employment thereby created for a period of six (6) months, commencing February 26, 1947, and you do hereby acknowledge the due and timely exercise of the aforesaid option.

You do hereby ratify and confirm your aforesaid contract of employment with us and all of the terms and provisions thereof as the same may have been heretofore amended and all of the terms and provisions of your aforesaid contract of employment with us shall remain in full force and effect except as hereinbefore amended.

If the foregoing is in accordance with your understanding of our agreement, will you kindly execute all copies of this letter and return the same to us for execution by our Company, at which time we will return one fully executed copy to you for your records.

Yours very truly,

TWENTIETH CENTURY-FOX FILM CORPORATION

By

Its Executive Manager

Commitment Approved
By
DATE
Form Approved
By
Date 2/21/47

ACCEPTED:

SHORT SHORTS

ASSIGNMENTS

George Archainbaud yesterday was set for his fifth straight direction chore for William Boyd on latter's new series of Hoppies. Latest will be tagged "Hoppy's Holiday."

Michael M. Spack will head men's wardrobe for William Cagney production, "The Stray Lamb."

Walter Thompson swings over to Enterprise from International to act as film editor on "Arch of Triumph." Marion Herwood is fashion designer for Ruth Warrick's costumes on same film.

Spencer Bennet and **Fred Brannon** will co-direct Republic serial, "Jesse James Rides Again," which rolls Sept. 20 under producer helming of Mike Frankovitch.

Carl Berger, Herman Schopp and **Bob Gough** handle cameras on Romay's "The Return of Rin Tin Tin," with J. Paul Skylos set as art director, **Eddie Mann** as editor and **Harold Knox**, assistant director.

Al Siegler set as cameraman on Columbia's "The Lone Wolf's Invitation to Murder."

Oren Haglund assigned as assistant director for Warner Bros.' "Night Unto Night."

Bernard Newman set as fashion designer on Warners' "Woman in White."

George Van Marter draws art director stint on Columbia's "Twin Sombreros."

Col. Clarence Shoop, commander of experimental base at Muroc during war and now organizing, as commandant, 146th Fighter Group of California Air National Guard, goes to Paramount as technical advisor on "Blaze of Noon."

Bert Briskin yesterday was set as first assistant director on Sol Lesser's "Tarzan and the Huntress." Harold Glendenning was put in charge of wardrobe, Irving Berns, makeup and Barney Smith, sound effects.

Gene Bryant yesterday was named production manager, **Saul Wurtzel** first assistant director and **Leon Shamroy,** cinematographer, for 20th-Fox's "Forever Amber."

Warren Lowe goes on Hal Wallis' "Desert Town" as film editor and Harry Lindgren draws sound stint.

NEW CONTRACTS

Howard Koch inked to term writing deal by Liberty.

Mark Lee Kirk, art director, option lifted by 20th-Fox.

Jane Ball and **Norma Jeane Dougherty** signed to new contracts by 20th-Fox.

John Payne hoisted by 20th-Fox.

Paul C. Lees was reoptioned yesterday as actor by Paramount.

...of Young
...erica Films, tomorrow.
Maxine Arto, of KFI production dept., and Jimmie McKibben, writer, were married at Las Vegas.

Unhitching
Aileen Pringle was awarded a divorce yesterday from James M. Cain.

...NG
...SKA
...6-6214

Left: Making her film debut, Marilyn is briefly glimpsed walking behind the young Natalie Wood and star, June Haver, in the 1948 release of *Scudda Hoo! Scudda Hay!*

Opposite: A fresh-faced, 20-year-old Marilyn.

Above: Norma Jeane Dougherty's first contract with Twentieth Century-Fox is noted in *Variety.* When it was renewed six months later (*left above*), the contract acknowledged the transformation of Norma Jeane to Marilyn Monroe.

SCREEN TESTS

In this 1950 screen test, Marilyn plays a gangster's girlfriend opposite Richard Conte. She was resigned by Twentieth Century-Fox on December 10th, 1950.

Opposite: Glamorous and sultry before the cameras, Marilyn appears opposite a young Robert Wagner in this screen test on June 14th, 1951.

STARLET DAYS

NEW YORK   LONDON   CHICAGO   BEVERLY HILLS

ESTABLISHED 1898

WILLIAM MORRIS AGENCY
INC.
ROCKEFELLER CENTER
1270 SIXTH AVENUE
NEW YORK 20, N.Y.
TELEPHONE CIRCLE 7-2160

AMERICAN FEDERATION OF RADIO ARTISTS

STANDARD AFRA EXCLUSIVE AGENCY CONTRACT

UNDER RULE 12-A

Beverly Hills, California

THIS AGREEMENT, made and entered into at_____, by and between

WILLIAM MORRIS AGENCY, INC., hereinafter called the "AGENT," and_____

Marilyn Monroe_____, hereinafter called the "ARTIST."

WITNESSETH:

1. The Artist employs the Agent as his sole and exclusive Agent in the broadcasting industry within the scope of the regulations of the American Federation of Radio Artists (hereinafter called AFRA), and agrees not to employ any other person or persons to act for him in like capacity during the term hereof, and the Agent accepts such employment. This contract is limited to the broadcasting industry and to contracts of the Artist as an artist in such field, and any reference hereinafter to contracts or employment whereby the Artist renders his services, refers to contracts or employment in the broadcasting industry, except as otherwise provided herein.

Note: This contract also includes the Artist's services for phonograph records and the term "broadcasting industry" shall also include the phonograph record field unless this sentence is stricken.

2. The Artist agrees that prior to any engagement or employment in the radio broadcasting industry, he will become a member of AFRA in good standing and remain such a member for the duration of such engagement or employment. The Artist warrants that he has the right to make this contract and that he is not under any other agency contract in the radio broadcasting field. The Agent warrants that he is and will remain a duly franchised agent of AFRA for the duration of this contract. This paragraph is for the benefit of AFRA and AFRA members as well as for the benefit of the parties to this agreement.

3. The term of this contract shall be for a period of _____three years_____, commencing the 2nd day of _____March_____ 194 9.

Note—The term may not be in excess of three years.

ten

4. (a) The Artist agrees to pay to the Agent a sum equal to _____per cent (not more than 10%) of all moneys or other consideration received by the Artist, directly or indirectly, under contracts of employment entered into during the term specified herein or in existence when this contract is entered into unless the Artist is obligated to pay commission on such existing employment contract to another Agent as provided in the Regulations. Commissions shall be payable when and as such moneys or other consideration are received by the Artist or by anyone else for or on the Artist's behalf.

(b) Any moneys or other consideration received by the Artist or by anyone for or on his behalf in connection with any termination of any contract of the Artist on which the Agent would otherwise be entitled to receive commission, or in connection with the settlement of any such contract, or any litigation arising out of such contract, shall also be moneys in connection with which the Agent is entitled to the aforesaid commissions; provided, however, that in such event the Artist shall be entitled to deduct arbitration fees, attorney's fees, expenses and court costs before computing the amount upon which the Agent is entitled to his commissions.

(c) Such commissions shall be payable by the Artist to the Agent, as aforesaid, during the term of this contract and thereafter only where specifically provided herein.

(d) The Agent shall be entitled to the aforesaid commissions after the expiration of the term specified herein, for so long a period thereafter as the Artist continues to receive moneys or other consideration under or upon employment contracts entered into by the Artist during the term specified herein, including moneys or other consideration received by the Artist under the extended term of such employment contracts, resulting from the exercise of

MS

328

the name, portraits and pictures of the Artist to representation of the Artist hereunder.

minimums established by AFRA under any collective

in matters which concern the professional interests

ist.

er commitment on behalf of the Artist, without the he terms and conditions (including compensation of

duciary. The Agent, when instructed in writing by ist's affairs, will not disclose such information.

ped, to represent the interests of the Artist ably his contract, and that he will so represent the Artist.

uring employment for the services of the Artist in

Beverly Hills, Calif.
telephone open during all reasonable business hours city of New York N.Y., or its environs, throughout the term of this agreement, and that some representative of the Agent will be present at such office during such business hours. This contract is void unless the blank in this paragraph is filled in with the name of a city at which the Agent does maintain an office for the radio broadcasting agency business.

(i) At the written request of the Artist, given to the Agent not oftener than once every four (4) weeks, the Agent shall give the Artist information in writing, stating what efforts the Agent has rendered on behalf of the Artist within a reasonable time preceding the date of such request.

(j) The Agent will not charge or collect any commissions on compensation received by the Artist for services rendered by the Artist in a package show in which the Agent is interested, where prohibited by Section VIII of AFRA's Regulations.

12. This contract is subject to AFRA's Regulations Governing Agents (Rule 12-A). Any controversy under this contract, or as to its existence, validity, construction, performance, non-performance, breach, operation, continuance or termination shall be settled by arbitration in accordance with the arbitration provisions in the Regulations.

(FOR CALIFORNIA ONLY)

This provision is inserted in this contract pursuant to a rule of AFRA, a bona fide labor union, which Rule regulates the relations of its members to employment agencies. Reasonable written notice shall be given to the Labor Commissioner of the State of California of the time and place of any arbitration hearing hereunder. The Labor Commissioner of the State of California, or his authorized representative, has the right to attend all arbitration hearings. The clauses relating to the Labor Commissioner of the State of California shall not be applicable to cases not falling under the provisions of Section 1647.5 of the Labor Code of the State of California.

Nothing in this contract nor in AFRA's Regulations Governing Agents (Rule 12-A) shall be construed so as to abridge or limit any rights, powers or duties of the Labor Commissioner of the State of California.

IN WITNESS WHEREOF, the parties hereto have executed this agreement the 2 day of March 494 9.

x _____Marilyn Monroe_____
Marilyn Monroe   ARTIST
WILLIAM MORRIS AGENCY, INC.

By _____
AGENT

NOTE: This contract must be signed at least in triplicate. One copy must be promptly delivered by the Agent to AFRA, one copy must be promptly delivered by the Agent to the Artist, and one copy must be retained by the Agent. If AFRA has an office in the city where the contract is executed, AFRA's copy of the contract must be delivered to that office within 10 days of execution; or at the Agent's option, to AFRA's main office in New York City within 20 days of execution.

This agency and Artists' Manager is licensed by the Labor Commissioner of the State of California.

This agency is franchised by the American Federation of Radio Artists.

This form of contract has been approved by the American Federation of Radio Artists.

This contract approved as to form by the Labor Commissioner of the State of California on November 22, 1946.

Above: The actress who never won an Academy Award, embraces one at the 1951 ceremonies.

A rare document, Marilyn's 1949 radio contract.

Opposite: In the make-up chair at Twentieth Century-Fox in 1952 where she will become 'Marilyn Monroe'. Without make-up, however, Marilyn always looked girlishly youthful.

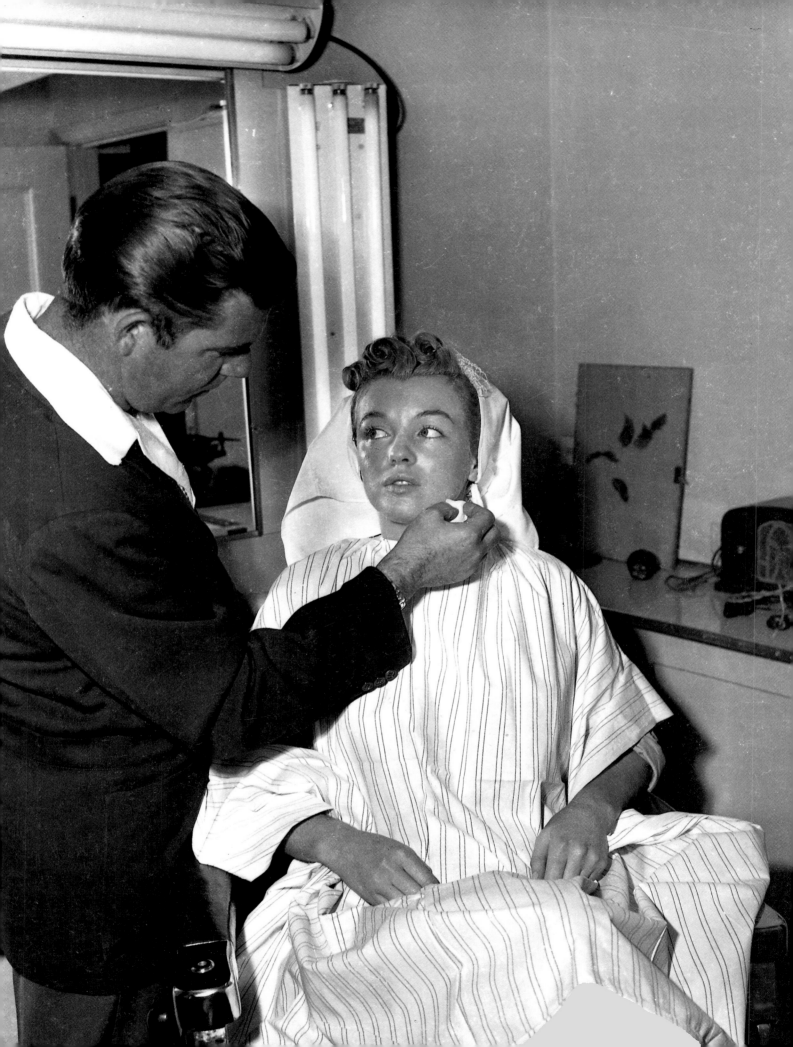

A warm welcome to the Claridge Hotel in Atlantic City, New Jersey, in September 1952, after an invitation to take part as 'Grand Marshal' in the Miss America pageant. Later she appeared in person at the Stanley Theatre (*right*) where her new film, *Monkey Business*, was showing that night.

ARRIVAL OF A STAR

Child actor, Tommy Rettig, lies at Marilyn's feet during a scene in *River of No Return*, which was filmed in 1953.

Opposite: Marilyn prepares to film her 'bath in the waterfall' sequence, which was subsequently cut from *River of No Return* prior to its 1954 release.

GOLDEN DREAMS

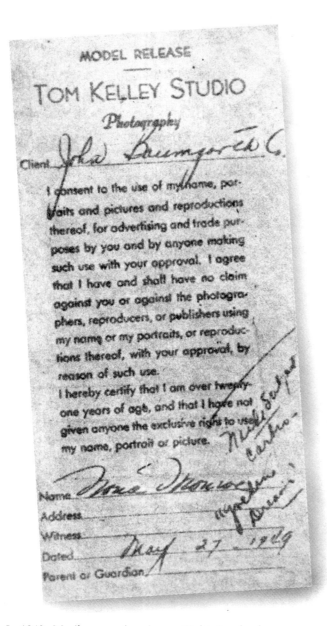

In 1949, Marilyn posed nude for photographer Tom Kelley, while she was still a struggling young actress, signing her model release to Kelley 'Mona Monroe'.

Right: A calendar manufacturer holds up two versions of the nude pose in his offerings for 1954, when Marilyn was the hottest property in Hollywood.

WITH THE TROOPS IN KOREA

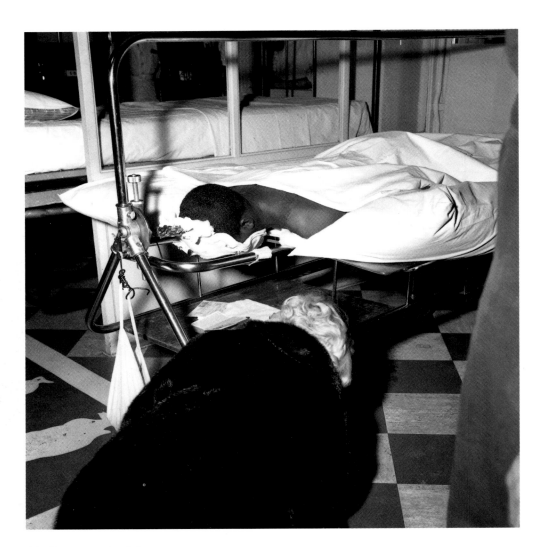

Opposite: Signing her 1948 pin-up poster pose for weary but delighted soldiers in Korea on January 18th, 1854.

Marilyn entertained the troops in Korea during 1954. Here she chats with a wounded soldier whose injuries prevented him from rising to greet her.

SIGHTINGS OF A LEGEND IN THE MAKING

The thing I'd like the most is to become a real actress. I remember when I was a kid at the movies on Saturday afternoon. I'd sit in the front row and I'd think how wonderful it would be to be an actress, you know. But I didn't really realize about acting. I appreciated what I saw. Bad, good, it didn't matter, I enjoyed it very much. Anything that would move on the screen. However, you know, I realize more and more the responsibility, and as I say, I would like to be a good actress.

MARILYN MONROE 1955

For me the story began when I was fourteen years old. A film, *Clash by Night*, came to the RKO 23rd Street Theatre, and what drew me to that film was that its star, Barbara Stanwyck, very much reminded me of my mother. In a featured role was a new actress named Marilyn Monroe. The film opened on August 6th, 1952, oddly enough, ten years to the very moment of Monroe's demise. I went to see *Clash by Night* on Saturday, August 8th, going in to see Barbara Stanwyck and coming out totally thrown by the buoyancy, the laughter, the considerable charm of this other person on the screen, with whom, I think it is safe to say, I remain in love to this very moment. That was the first time I saw her.

In addition to *Clash by Night*, between 1951 and 1953 Marilyn Monroe could be seen on movie screens in such cinema fare as *As Young as You Feel, Love Nest, Let's Make It Legal, We're Not Married, Don't Bother to Knock, Monkey Business, O. Henry's Full House, Niagara* (a personal favorite of mine even today; the onset of genuine movie stardom for Monroe), and *Gentlemen Prefer Blondes*.

Soon after the release of *Gentlemen Prefer Blondes*, Monroe made her live small-screen debut on television's *The Jack Benny Show*, during which, in addition to performing in a comedy skit with Jack, she sang 'Bye Bye Baby' from *Blondes*. A decade later, Marilyn-clone Jayne Mansfield was destined to repeat the Monroe-Benny comedy skit when she appeared on Benny's show on November 26th, 1963. I fondly recall,

Having seen Marilyn for the first time in *Clash By Night* on August 9th, 1952, I wrote to her studio requesting a photograph. This was the portrait I received in 1953, inscribed: 'To Jimmy, warmest regards, Marilyn Monroe'.

This was the movie
advertisement that led me
towards a journey with
Marilyn Monroe, which
continued through the last
eight years of her life.

back in 1953, making out with my girlfriend Doreen while watching Marilyn's romp with Benny, telecast that September 15th. In lieu of payment, Jack gave Marilyn a black Cadillac convertible (in which I would subsequently photograph her) for her small-screen effort.

I wrote a letter to Twentieth Century-Fox Studios around that period, to Marilyn Monroe, requesting a signed photograph from their new star. Seven weeks later a manila envelope arrived; in it was an 8 × 10-inch portrait of Marilyn with an inscription written in red ink: 'To Jimmy, Warmest regards, Marilyn Monroe.'

Then something terrific happened. It was reported in the press that Monroe would be coming to New York City to film location scenes for *The Seven Year Itch*. Marilyn was due to arrive in the city on September 8th, 1954, and on that day I went to what was then called Idlewild Airport (now Kennedy Airport). At that time there was a main terminal, above which was an outdoor ramp that ran perhaps the length of two city blocks, and you could view the entire airfield from that particular spot. This was the era when planes would land and portable staircases would be rolled up to the front door, and passengers would exit down those staircases onto the airfield. I spent that entire day watching every plane that landed, keenly watching every passenger that got off. At no time did Monroe appear, so, feeling very disappointed, sometime late that night I returned home.

The following morning I had the television set on and they were interrupting programming to show Monroe who had now arrived. During the course of that same day, some form of media advised that she was staying at the St Regis Hotel, at 55th Street and Fifth Avenue. Finally, she was here!

The very next morning I made my way to the St Regis Hotel, coming upon a substantial number of people outside waiting to see Marilyn. In my own very reticent, very shy way, I preferred to stay on the other side of the street. I walked up and down in the sunshine for most of the day, fully aware that if Marilyn appeared I would hear some kind of noise from the crowd and know that she was there. By evening I was on the same side of the street as the crowd and the hotel – small miracle! The hotel had two entrances, separated by about fifteen feet. I was at one entrance, the crowd at the other; maybe they knew something I didn't? In any event, at 7 p.m. that night, September 10th, 1954, I heard the crowd suddenly roar, looked over and saw a commotion, and realized that 'she' had to be there! With a surge of urgency overwhelming me, I made my way into the crowd and, for all my very real shyness, literally separated the people in it until I got right up to the object of their (my!) affection.

I was startled, because all that day I'd expected to see a woman wearing a flame-red dress and hoop earrings, with tousled blonde hair, and 'larger than life'; the image of Monroe from *Niagara*. Instead, I found myself looking downwards (I am six feet tall) at this incredibly beautiful face, framed by perfectly combed hair. She was wearing not a tight red dress, but an elegant black dress, full-skirted, which went outwards from her body, concealing the lower portions of her oh-so-famous figure. Instead of stiletto high heels, she had on very low cuban heels. She was looking down because she was signing somebody's autograph book. I looked down into her face, and the first word that came into my head was 'Angel' – she looked like an angel to me. Instead of being fascinated, I was smitten. Smitten, hell; I was all at once in love! Monroe finished signing autographs and managed to get herself into a taxicab. As she closed the cab door, she advised the worshipping crowd: 'I'll be back at nine o'clock.'

I was back at the St Regis Hotel at ten minutes to nine. I was not then, nor have I ever been, an autograph collector, and I didn't own a camera. People clustered around her begging autographs and taking snapshots. I was just staring at her. With that shyness that I had one more time tucked aside, when they had finished with her, I looked at her and asked, 'Miss Monroe, would you give me a kiss?' She looked back at me and there was 'No' written all over her face. Never one to be put off when something is really important to me, I sort of tapped the side of my face; 'Here, just on

Norma Jeane Mortenson had certainly come a long way. *Gentlemen Prefer Blondes* co-star, Jane Russell, joins Marilyn in implanting their imprints in the forecourt at Grauman's Chinese Theatre, Hollywood, in June 1953.

the cheek, please?' There was a little chorus of 'oohs' and 'aahs' from the crowd – they were obviously living vicariously – and the next thing I knew, Marilyn put her arms around me and kissed me!

The following night Marilyn emerged from a car dressed in a royal blue jumpsuit, stiletto high heels, a mink coat draped over her shoulders, and with her blonde hair worn down to her shoulders. She looked sensational. A little boy (remember, at this time I was sixteen), who may have been eight or nine years old, asked, 'Marilyn, can I have a kiss?' She looked down at him and answered very sweetly: 'No, I can't,' adding, 'Joe', an obvious reference to her then husband Joe DiMaggio. When that happened, I just felt it was extraordinary that I'd managed a kiss from her on the previous night. Clearly, she wasn't frivolous about kissing strangers, so this became quite a moment for me.

The next night, September 12th, I was back at the hotel and struck up a conversation with a fan waiting there with his camera in hand. By this time I had bought myself a camera; we agreed that we would attempt to sneak into the hotel and, if we were at all lucky in getting to Marilyn (I already knew that she was staying in Suite 1105–6), I would use his camera to take pictures of him with her and he would do the same for me with mine. And so it was that two timid-feeling kids walked quietly into the lobby of the prestigious St Regis Hotel and somehow managed to get to a staircase and climb all the way up to the eleventh floor! Trembling somewhat, we proceeded to the end of the hallway and rang her door buzzer. A man opened the door. I asked if we could 'see Miss Monroe?' He answered, 'Wait here a minute,' and closed the door. He came back and said, 'No, I'm sorry, you can't see her.'

Dejected, we decided to return to the lobby on the elevator. Just as we had pressed the 'down' button, the elevator door opened and who stepped off but Joe DiMaggio! Meeting the moment, I pushed my shyness aside one more time and asked, 'Excuse me, Mr DiMaggio. Is it at all possible that we could meet Miss Monroe?' We were all

A pause in the filming of *The Seven Year Itch*, just days after I was granted my first kiss from Marilyn.

Tom Ewell, co-star of *The Seven Year Itch*, witnesses cinema history in the making as Marilyn Monroe's dress billows skywards in this famous scene for *The Seven Year Itch*. I was one of thousands of New Yorkers who watched the location filming after midnight on September 15th, 1954. Joe DiMaggio, also in the crowd that night, was visibly unhappy with his wife's public display.

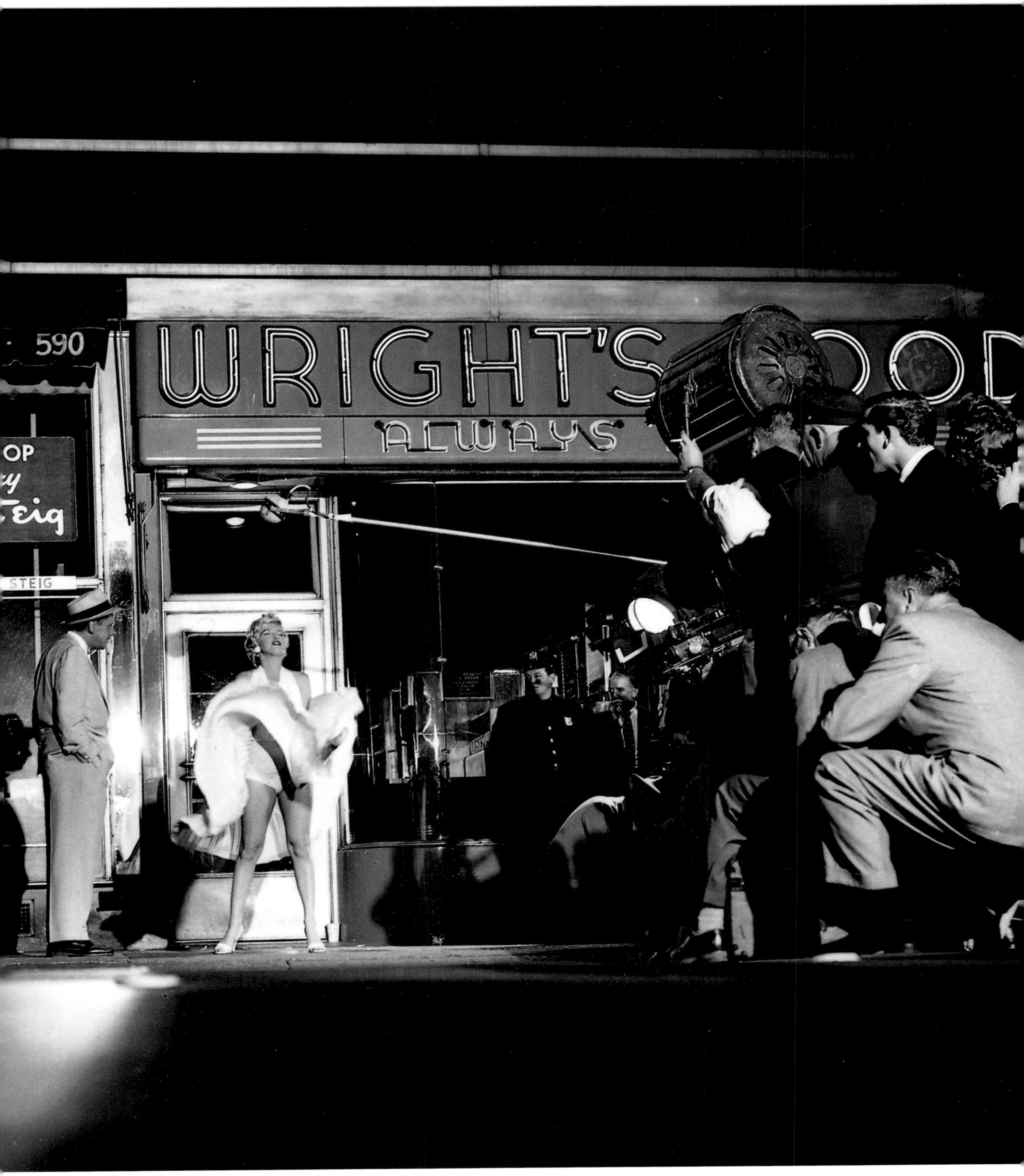
590
WRIGHT'S
ALWAYS
OP
Teig
STEIG

268 CERTIFICATE OF REGISTRY OF MARRIAGE ВООК 1074 195

(PERSONAL DATA LICENSE TO MARRY CERTIFICATION OF MARRIAGE)

GROOM PERSONAL DATA

Name of Groom: Joseph Paul Di Maggio — Age of Groom: 39

Usual Residence of Groom: 2150 Beach — San Francisco — S.F.

Birthplace: Calif.

Color or Race: White — Divorced — 1

Name of Father of Groom: Joseph Di Maggio — Italy — Maiden Name of Mother of Groom: Rosalie Mercurio — Italy

BRIDE PERSONAL DATA

Name of Bride: Norma Jeane Dougherty — Age of Bride: 25

Usual Residence of Bride: 882 No. Doheney Dr. — Los Angeles — L.A.

Birthplace: Calif.

Color or Race: White — Divorced — 1

Name of Father of Bride: Edward Mortenson — unknown — Gladys Monroe — Mexico

Maiden Name of Bride if previously married: Norma Jean Mortenson

LICENSE TO MARRY: Norma Jeane Mortenson Dougherty — Joseph P. Di Maggio

County of Issue of License: San Francisco — JAN 14 1954 — 8595

CERTIFICATION OF PERSON PERFORMING CEREMONY AND WITNESS: January 14 '54 — San Francisco, California

Address of Witness: 3789 F Elmore St. San Francisco, Calif.

Signature of Person Performing Ceremony: Charles T. Peery, Municipal Judge, San Francisco, Calif.

LOCAL REGISTRAR: JAN 15 1954 — San Francisco County

IN THE SUPERIOR COURT OF THE STATE OF CALIFORNIA
IN AND FOR THE COUNTY OF LOS ANGELES

NORMA JEANE DI MAGGIO,
    Plaintiff,

vs.

JOSEPH PAUL DI MAGGIO,
    Defendant.

NO. S.M. D- 12391

COMPLAINT FOR DIVORCE
(Cruelty)

Comes now the plaintiff and for cause of action against the defendant alleges as follows:

4. That the time elapsing from the date of marriage to the date of separation of the parties is: Eight (8) months and thirteen (13) days.

5. That there is no issue of said marriage.

That there is no community property.

V

That each of the parties hereto is self-supporting.

VI

That since the marriage of the parties defendant has inflicted upon plaintiff grievous mental cruelty, causing her grievous mental suffering and anguish, all of which acts and conduct on the part of defendant were without the fault of plaintiff, and by reason of which defendant has caused plaintiff grievous mental distress, suffering and anguish.

---

walking down the hallway towards 'that' door again. Before entering, Joe answered, 'Well, wait here and I'll see.' A minute later he opened the door and brought her out, then went back inside; DiMaggio just left her there with us. We were amazed, of course. I took a picture of this other kid with Marilyn and he did the same for me with my camera. I then grabbed a couple of shots of Marilyn alone, and she returned to her suite.

Downstairs there were, it seemed, a thousand people waiting outside the hotel. Monroe's appearance in New York City had caused a sensation. When she finally left the hotel with DiMaggio, I remember that the crowd on the sidewalk was so dense that a woman was actually standing on the roof of a taxicab. Monroe and DiMaggio were standing at the top of the hotel's outer staircase, trying to figure out how they were going to get from there into the taxicab, when the roof of this cab started to give way under the weight of the woman, who just sort of toppled into my arms. She was destined to re-enter my life the following year in a more reasonable fashion.

Three nights later, Marilyn made cinema history when she emerged from the Trans Lux 52nd Street Theatre on Lexington Avenue and walked towards a subway grating, over which her white pleated skirt billowed skywards – a key scene in *The Seven Year*

Above left: The marriage certificate of Marilyn and Joe DiMaggio. DiMaggio adored Marilyn but his possessiveness put too big a strain on the marriage, which was dissolved eight months later (*above right*).

Overleaf: Marilyn sits surrounded by Milton Greene, Irving Berlin, Joan Collins, Bing Crosby, Olivia DeHavilland, Mona Freeman, Judy Garland, Joseph Mankiewicz, Donald O'Connor, Ann Sothern, et al, at this 1954 studio screening room presentation of *There's No Business Like Show Business,* following which, she failed to show at the film's premiere in New York City.

Itch. Italian movie star Gina Lollobrigida was making her first appearance in New York (in a previous film of hers, *Crossed Swords,* she had been publicly billed as 'Italy's Marilyn Monroe'), and she was brought over to the Trans Lux to meet Monroe. Filming of Marilyn's scene got underway shortly after midnight, and they shot footage for the next five hours, most of that time consumed with studio people manipulating the Press into what swiftly became a worldwide media image: Marilyn standing with her legs akimbo atop a New York City subway grating with her skirt blowing up. Joe DiMaggio was standing on the sidelines watching some of this.

I must confess, I had no trouble seeing through Marilyn's sheer panties. Actually, she had two pairs of panties on, but still I had no trouble seeing through them. Most of the published photographs from that night do not illustrate this intimacy. I think they shot the scene fifteen times, so it was a very exciting, intimate situation being played out over and over again before my eyes! Nonetheless, I could fully appreciate DiMaggio's anger. Indeed, Joe stood there sour-faced. In defence of Monroe, I am reasonably convinced that in her dressing room she did not see what the powerful Kleig lights then put on display for what the Press later called 'five thousand onlookers'. And there were people everywhere. I recall for a time watching the action while sitting on the roof of a four-storey building across the way. But having spent a good portion of the night standing alongside the impressive Cinemascope movie camera that was recording the scene, I appear in numerous photographs of the crowd taken that memorable night.

During this period I was employed at the Globe Mail Agency, then located at 148 West 23rd Street. To this very day, if you go across the street to 155 West 23rd Street, there remains a big square of sidewalk cement in which, some thirty-six years ago, I scribbled in large lettering: 'Marilyn Monroe Was Here'.

My 1954 notice to fellow New Yorkers that 'Marilyn Monroe was here' can still be seen today in the cement outside 155 West 23rd Street.

My next opportunity to see Monroe in person was on December 16th, when the New York City premiere of her film *There's No Business Like Show Business* was to take place at the Roxy Theatre. I had gone to a movie premiere for *The Last Time I Saw Paris* only weeks before, attended by its star, Elizabeth Taylor, for which my ticket cost $2.75. Well, tickets for the *Show Business* premiere were priced at $10.00 each, somewhat outrageous for the time. I was then making a salary of $28.00 a week! Even so, I was so certain that Monroe would be there in person that I bought a ticket to her premiere – and found myself sitting next to Zsa Zsa Gabor for my ten bucks. Marilyn never showed. Three weeks later it would be a different story.

On the evening of January 7th, 1955, Marilyn appeared at the house of her lawyer, Frank Delaney, at 59 East 64th Street. She was there with her new 'business partner', photographer Milton Greene, to meet with the Press in order to announce the onset of her cinematic independence with the formation of Marilyn Monroe Productions. (The only film they produced, ultimately, was *The Prince and the Showgirl*.) I was present that evening and met a young man named John Reilly, who would later become one of a half-dozen avid fans calling themselves 'the Monroe Six'. Subsequently the best man at my wedding in 1966, godfather to my offspring, Reilly is still my friend. Anyway, the door to number 59 opened, and I remember that some kind of a 'Countess' welcomed us in. The townhouse was mobbed with reporters and guests, and within minutes I found myself photographing Marilyn as she spoke with Marlene Dietrich at the gathering that night. Later, after I had departed, Dietrich invited Monroe, Milton Greene and his wife Amy back to her apartment on Park Avenue. John Reilly was there in the wee hours of the morning when the trio arrived at Dietrich's building. As Monroe entered the elevator with the Greenes, Reilly shot a photograph of Marilyn standing to the side wall of the cubicle. Her lips closed, she is looking incredibly sad; there almost appears to be a tear in her eye (she was more likely simply fatigued). In retrospect, it is one of the most beautiful pictures ever taken of the legendary Monroe.

John later told me that Marilyn was 'drunk' by that hour of the morning; there had obviously been a lot of celebrating over the formation of Marilyn Monroe Productions. I should clarify here that in eight years of seeing Marilyn frequently, I never saw her drunk, not even tipsy. Sometime later I showed Marilyn the photograph and advised, 'This was taken in an elevator in Marlene Dietrich's apartment building, and you were "very high!"' Without even a pause, a wide-eyed Marilyn looked intently into my face and inquired, 'What floor was I on?' It was a classic response, and it was all mine!

Reflecting on New York City, Marilyn said, 'This will be my home from now on.' And so it was. On January 19th, with newly divorced ex-husband Joe DiMaggio's assistance, Monroe moved into a small, unpretentious hotel on East 52nd Street, just west of Lexington Avenue, the Gladstone. The building was razed years later; there now stands a towering office building where the Gladstone Hotel once sat. Of course, in time the Press always allowed you to know where Monroe was staying: I discovered she was now living at the Gladstone. I recall the first evening I saw her there, January 26th. The Press was literally outside the door wherever Monroe was, and there was a lot of Press there that night. Marilyn came out of the elevator and I remember she had gloves on, little sort of netted gloves. There was a small room off the hotel's main entrance, a lobby room with couches and chairs, where the Press was photographing her. They had her pick up a telephone receiver and pretend to be talking into it. In fact, the instrument was disconnected. The very next day there appeared newspaper pictures of 'Marilyn on the telephone with Joe', alongside a picture of DiMaggio himself on yet another phone. But when these photos were taken, Monroe was not actually talking to DiMaggio; it was my very first lesson as regards accuracy in the media. But then, being in proximity to Marilyn over the next years would afford me many lessons to come!

A professional photographer in the room – it may have been Sam Shaw, who later became a friend of Monroe's – asked for my help with something, handing him flashbulbs, I think. When the whole thing came to a conclusion, I preceded Marilyn

Below left: Marilyn, who was now living in New York, gleefully holds up the first snapshot of herself with me, which I had just presented to her in January 1955.

Below right: Photographer Sam Shaw and I with a ghost-like Marilyn in 1955.

outside, and as she came through the hotel's revolving door, I raised my arm in her direction and requested, 'Well, at least shake my hand.' She extended her net-gloved hand, we shook, and the next thing I knew she was gone, like always.

That February 28th, she emerged from the Gladstone wearing a figure-hugging sleek black cocktail dress, a mink coat slung over her shoulders, and what I've always referred to as her 'Garbo hat' – a black kind of bowl-shaped hat. Marilyn got into a taxicab, and I had my five-dollar camera with me and captured one of my most sensationally beautiful colour images of her; a flawless profile taken as she sat in the back seat of the cab, just a glorious picture. She looked smashing that night.

The next time I saw her at the hotel she was with the photographer Sam Shaw, and on this particular evening her hair looked exactly like straw! That was still in February. Shaw and I posed for a photograph with her that night in which she appears eerily ghost-like. It is a fascinating picture. Sam and Marilyn, myself between them, and she is absolutely aglow; so much so that you can barely see her. Something happened that night between Monroe and the lens; Shaw and I are perfectly fine in the picture and Marilyn is truly ethereal-looking.

Arriving at Elizabeth Arden's salon on Fifth Avenue. Marilyn's walk there from her apartment at the Gladstone Hotel caused traffic chaos!

On a mild mid-morning shortly there-after, I was walking towards the Gladstone and as I arrived at the entrance I came upon a teenager standing outside with an 8-mm movie camera aimed directly at the hotel's revolving door, which was already in motion. Marilyn came awhirl through the door and literally performed a 360-degree turn for his home-movie camera. She was dressed in an elegant black suit with a fur collar, her lustrous hair shoulder length, and she was fully made up. Dazzling! She was about to walk from 52nd Street and Lexington Avenue over to the Fifth Avenue beauty salon of Elizabeth Arden. So I walked side by side with her; naturally, to the utter frustration of this kid who was walking backwards with his movie camera pointed at us, because I was now unavoidably in all of his wonderful footage of Marilyn. In fact, although I sought him out over the following years, he never allowed me to see the candid film he took of Marilyn and me walking across town that day.

As she walked her famous walk in her very high black stiletto heels, cars and trucks just pulled over to the curb and drivers emerged from them shouting 'Marilyn! Marilyn!' When we finally got the three blocks over to Fifth Avenue, we then had to walk uptown to 54th–55th Streets. As we arrived at the doorway to Elizabeth Arden's salon, I heard the nearby sounds of an automobile crashing, and looked over to see a taxicab driver whose head was bobbing out of the passenger-side front window of his cab, the vehicle itself now embedded in the back end of a delivery truck! He had a gleeful smile on his face and was hollering, 'Marilyn!' I tapped her on the shoulder and exclaimed 'See what you did!' She gave me a very 'Marilynesque' laugh and swept rather grandly into the salon.

I guess it is time to clarify that the Marilyn Monroe who was known to the movie-going public of that era was something of a missing person to me, because the individual who was there in front of me at these times was so different; she was not at all the personage visible on the motion-picture screens. But arriving at Elizabeth Arden's, Marilyn was in her full-movie star persona, and playing that to the very hilt, which was great fun for me to see her do. It was as if when Norma Jeane applied the make-up, 'Marilyn' emerged, and this only served to make the woman even more intriguing, be that at all possible.

Soon came the announcement Monroe would be 'an usherette' at the March 9th world premiere of the James Dean film, *East of Eden*, opening at the Astor Theatre. That night at the Gladstone I came upon wooden police horses set up on both sides of the entrance to the hotel, holding back hundreds of Monroe admirers. In addition, there was a long line of people that wrapped around onto Park Avenue, fans who had cameras and autograph books awaiting the Monroe image and signature. With her limousine sitting at the curb, what had been arranged for the more ambitious fans was that when Monroe came down in the elevator these people would be allowed to go one at a time to the elevator door and either take a snapshot or obtain an autograph.

Little by little, finally everyone had been serviced, as it were, and I got on the end of that line and was the last person to reach the door of the elevator. With a feeling of dismay that I didn't have my camera along, I walked right into the cubicle, looped my arm through hers, and said, 'I'll take you out to the car, Marilyn.' She was wearing an off-white brocade gown with a fur-trimmed stole, I was dressed in jeans and a black leather jacket. We must have been a sight and a half!

At the 1955 premiere of *East of Eden*, in the Astor Theatre, New York, during which Marilyn acted as 'usherette'.

Opposite: Marilyn's elephant ride at New York City's Madison Square Garden proved to be a painful one – it turned out that a pin had been left in the seat of her newly-made costume – but, a true professional, she carried on without visible complaint.

As we came through the hotel's revolving doors, probably seventy-five or so flashbulbs exploded into a virtual sea of bright light, yet I have never seen even a single photograph taken of that moment. I escorted Marilyn to the limo, helped her inside and closed the car door. Having just usurped his job, I then noted her chauffeur standing there quite mute. I went around to the other side of the car to look at Marilyn through the window. Although she was to me consistently, incredibly beautiful, there were a few moments, this being one of them, when Marilyn was so outrageously gorgeous that it was actually hard to look at her. But I did.

She went on to the premiere, and the word quickly spread throughout Times Square that 'Marilyn Monroe is over at the Astor Theatre!' Soon people in the thousands picked up that information along Broadway. Marilyn was going to a post-premiere party at the Astor Roof atop the Astor Hotel, directly across the street from the movie theatre. By the film's conclusion, there was no way to move along that block bridging the theatre and the hotel. To one side of the hotel, next to an entrance, was a very large display window with a healthy-sized cement sill that I managed to take refuge on. Side doors to the theatre were opened, and celebrities like Sammy Davis Jr came walking through the crowd, and were welcomed and shouted at and applauded. One by one the celebrities came across, and then the doors were closed again, with everybody still there waiting for Marilyn. As if on cue, at exactly midnight the doors reopened and you could see about eleven or twelve policemen and a tousled blonde head in the middle of them. It was no small task getting Marilyn across that

On the way to meet her date – a pink elephant at the Mike Todd Circus Benefit – on the night of March 30th, 1955.

jammed street. I remember more than one person suddenly pirouetting out of the crowd, screaming hysterically 'I touched her! I touched her!' When she got up close to where I was, heading for the entrance to the hotel, she was out of breath. I gazed at her face and there were tears streaming down her cheeks with the joy and exhilaration, the excitement and love that was happening all around her. I didn't go into the hotel, but someone who did told me there were people in the Ladies Room standing in line outside the bathroom stall that Marilyn took refuge in, passing papers and pens underneath the stall for her to sign!

Monroe was set to ride a pink elephant in Madison Square Garden for a Mike Todd Circus Benefit on March 30th. I bought a ticket in the next-to-last row, which subsequently seemed about a mile away from the action, but it was all I could afford at the time. What happened behind the scenes that evening was that Marilyn had had a costume made for this event and then decided that she didn't like the way it photographed, so a new costume was fashioned, which arrived literally within minutes of when it was needed. Milton Berle was the evening's MC, and he advised the crowded arena, 'Here comes the only girl in the world who makes Jane Russell look like a boy!', at which point Marilyn was hoisted onto the back of the pink elephant – and a straight pin still in the bottom of the new costume instantly penetrated her buttocks! It took the elephant twenty-two minutes to circle the circus ring, and Monroe smiled and waved at patrons packed to the Garden's rafters, all the time bleeding from the puncture in her rear; a total professional.

Around April, Monroe moved out of the Gladstone and into the Waldorf Towers, where she sublet Suite 2728, then belonging to a woman named Leonora Corbett. By now there were appearing with a certain frequency

I had just turned seventeen when this photograph was taken with Marilyn in March 1955.

Taken in the Gladstone Hotel. Marilyn was truly so beautiful, that I could not take my eyes off her.

a half-dozen extremely avid Monroe fans who had met each other at her doorways and dubbed themselves 'the Monroe Six'. In addition to the aforementioned John Reilly, the group included one Gloria Milone (the very woman who had toppled off the roof of a taxicab and into my arms the previous September); a sister and brother, Eileen and Jimmy Collins; a soon to be sometimes girlfriend of mine, Edith Pitts; and yet another woman, Frieda Hull. Arriving from different parts of the surrounding areas, and as diverse a gathering of souls as one might imagine, both privately and professionally, over the next seasons the Six would ultimately monitor most of Monroe's comings and goings, resulting in numerous personal encounters with their elected idol. In time, Marilyn would come to refer to these special fans on a first name basis, and in turn, the Monroe Six dubbed Marilyn 'Mazzie'. There was an afternoon when a couple of the Six were near the door to Suite 2728 and overheard 'Mazzie' using the expletive 'Shit!' I only include this bit of trivia to humanize Monroe; during the entire eight years I knew Marilyn, I never heard her utter a single profanity.

One afternoon Marilyn exited the Waldorf Towers wearing a beige polo coat, her casual-looking hair worn rather long. She walked up to the corner, passing by a woman who was carrying a large bag of groceries and had a small female child toddling alongside her. Marilyn hailed a taxicab, and as she opened the cab door to get in, the woman recognized her and dropped the grocery bag. Without seeming to realize that her food items were now strewn about the sidewalk, the woman picked up the little girl, pressed the child's nose to the window of the cab and exclaimed excitedly 'Look! It's Marilyn Monroe! How adorable!' Marilyn's audience knew no boundaries.

REALITIES AND MYTHS

On a warm day in May, I encountered a sun-glassed Marilyn with Peter Leonardi, her hairdresser-chauffeur. One genuinely nice guy, Pete even took her clothes to the cleaners! On this particular day they emerged from the Towers toting a bicycle. Pete drove a beat-up red Ford convertible, and they threw the bicycle into the back seat of his car, resting it alongside Leonardi's own bike. They were going to drive in the car to Brooklyn's crowd-attracting Coney Island, bike ride around that area, then have a repast at Nathan's famed hot-dog stand. We took a bunch of candid snapshots that day, just prior to Marilyn and Pete's journey-in-anonymity to Coney Island.

Monroe's new film, *The Seven Year Itch* was previewed at the Loew's State Theatre in Times Square on June 1st. I didn't attend. Monroe did. Obviously, the movie-going crowd, elated about that, didn't miss me at all! The movie opened on June 3rd. There is a scene in *Itch*, the first 'dream' sequence in the film, where Marilyn comes down a flight of stairs, walks through a doorway, leans on a piano, and in a very breathy voice says, 'Rachmaninoff'. Well, the Monroe Six and I had a dispute over this scene; did she say 'Rachmaninoff' (also spelled Rachmaninov), or did she say 'Rock, my love'? We couldn't come to terms on this, so one afternoon when I encountered Marilyn in the garage of the Waldorf Towers, I asked her about it. Marilyn still had the black Cadillac convertible she had received from Jack Benny back in 1953 and had had the car brought to New York. She was now sitting on the passenger side with the door open, facing me with her legs still out of the car, wearing white pedal pushers and a sleeveless black top. She wore no make-up, only some hormone cream on her face. I asked her if she had said 'Rock, my love'?

Instead of articulating a simple 'No' answer, Marilyn opted to do the scene for me, much to my surprise. Tilting her head backwards, rolling it a half-turn, and breathlessly murmuring, 'Rachmaninoff!' Given the contrast of the high-gloss movie screen image of a gowned and fully made-up Monroe nestling inside my head, laid against that of the little virginal-faced peasant girl Norma Jeane sitting in front of me recreating the

I had longed to photograph Marilyn without her make-up, capturing her natural beauty. Relaxed and informal, she allowed me to take this picture as I aimed my camera from the ground (which explains why she appears to have a double chin!).

Marilyn had such zest for life, she was a joy to spend time with. These candid pictures taken in mid-1955 show the Marilyn I knew from day-to-day.

very same scene, it was truly a wonderful and fascinating moment spent with Marilyn. Eight months down the road she would play yet another movie scene, this one 'with' me, and a full quarter of a century would pass before I realized that it had happened.

Meanwhile, still in June, my next Monroe event of any note took place. I now had a Kodak Duaflex camera, this one a mite better than my previous five-dollar camera. With the Duaflex you could use either a number five or number twenty-five flashbulb; they were very large in size, and produced extremely bright flashes. I had long wanted to photograph Marilyn without her make-up on. Without the artificiality, she was really so wonderful looking. On this particular night, she was away taking an acting lesson at Lee Strasberg's apartment. In addition to the acting sessions she was attending at the Actors Studio, she took private lessons from Lee at home. When she returned from Strasberg's to the Waldorf Towers, she was wearing a little polka-dot bare-midriff blouse, white pedal pushers, a white raincoat and white flat shoes. No make-up, no hormone cream, absolutely nothing on her fabulous face. With a certain eagerness, I asked, 'Marilyn, would you please let me take a picture of you now? Just one, please?', and she answered, 'Alright, Jimmy'. As I shot the picture, the bulb produced

its not easy on the eye, very bright flash. Having been given that little go ahead, I then overstepped the boundaries; I had eleven flashbulbs with me, I shot eleven pictures!

This leads me to what took place the next day, an event which I think was really very telling. One has to review a bit of the Monroe history here. Monroe, her persona, her character, usually didn't permit her to react to people. I shouldn't put it quite that strongly; I think the person had to matter to her in order

Marilyn sets off to bike ride around Coney Island, with Peter Leonardi, her hairdresser–chauffeur (in background).

for her to react to them. The last-known time that she had publicly reacted in a retaliatory fashion was in the early 1950s when she was first receiving a lot of publicity. Marilyn had worn a certain dress to some show business function, and a very catty female reporter had taken her to task in print for having worn the garment. Another reporter opined to Monroe, 'If she had written that about me, I would have scratched her eyes out!' Monroe was reported to have answered: 'I thought it was crueller to leave her face exactly as it was.' Now this was the end of any kind of quote like that emanating from Marilyn Monroe. In later years, about the time of filming *Some Like It Hot*, Tony Curtis said to the reporter who asked what it was like to kiss Monroe, 'Kissing Marilyn was like kissing Hitler'. When Monroe was asked about this later on, she answered, 'There was this actor who said about me . . .' She didn't name the actor, she didn't name the film. In effect, she answered without malice; in essence, with almost a kind of dignity.

In any event, on this particular afternoon, following the night-of-the-eleven-flash-bulbs, I was walking directly behind Marilyn in the Waldorf garage when suddenly she swung around, pointed a firm finger at me, and said very sternly, 'I could have slapped your face last night!' I was dismayed that she should say this to me, but then I thought about it later on and realized that it was a kind of acceptance of me on her part. I didn't realize, as it was happening, that in reality she was comfortable enough with me to say that directly to me. It was very revealing, because if she had not by this time 'connected' with me, somehow she wouldn't have bothered to react that way. Marilyn was seizing the moment to admonish me for having offended her, which is really one of the signs of an on-going relationship. So, I viewed her actions in the broader scope, so to speak.

The Strasberg family, Lee and Paula and their children Susan and Johnny, were then living in a building called The Belnord, at 225 West 86th Street. This was where Monroe went for her evening lessons with Lee. In the summer of 1955, it was the

One night in June 1955, while she was on her way home from an acting lesson with Lee and Paula Strasberg, I asked Marilyn if I could take one picture with my new camera. Much to her annoyance, I then took eleven!

fashion for women to wear backless high–heeled shoes, and on this night Marilyn was wearing same along with a sleeveless dress that had brown and white horizontal stripes on it, thick brown leather belt, and a shoulder bag. Tanned and with some make-up on her face, she really did look totally incredible. As she left the apartment building, not knowing that I was there, she started walking eastward on 86th Street, fully visible to passers-by – 'Marilyn Monroe . . . there's Marilyn Monroe!' On this hot summer night, and attracted by that sensational walk of hers, three guys driving by in a convertible did a U-turn when they spotted her and began to pursue her loudly, honking their horn and making what amounted to rude, sexually tainted comments. Marilyn was trying her best to ignore them. Not infrequently it was her habit to walk home alone from here, the Towers being some forty-one blocks away. I'm not suggesting that she was going to trek all the way home this night, but she obviously felt like walking some. Well, a block and a half later, the guys were still there in that car, harassing her. She walked across the street, and I decided it was time to make my presence known. She was standing in front of a luncheonette called Bickford's, and obviously wanting a taxicab in order to extricate herself from this unfortunate situation. I went over to her and said, 'Marilyn, I see what's going on here, I'll get you a cab . . .', and she said, 'I'd appreciate that, Jimmy.' The menacing car had just made yet another

About to embark on a car trip from the garage of the Waldorf Towers.

U-turn and I guess my presence there beside Marilyn made a difference of some kind to these guys. They suddenly quietened down as I hailed a taxicab and protectively ushered Marilyn into its back-seat safety zone.

At around that time, this personage who had such high visibility actually found a place she could go to where the general public didn't readily recognize her. That happened to be down to the New York City Bowery. Now you see them on every corner, but back then the only place that you might see a derelict or an inebriated person lying in the gutter was 'down on the Bowery'. Peter Leonardi told me about this time, that she would have him drive her down to the Bowery, and they would walk along those streets where she would give handouts of money to these people. I think probably one of the pluses in it for her was that they were not looking back at 'Marilyn Monroe', so she was able to do something very humane within the boundaries of anonymity, which wasn't going to be bragged about for the rest of time by the people to whom it had happened. People-wise, it was just a one-on-one situation: 'Can I help you out a little bit?' So Pete would empty his pockets of all the money he had, then he would have to wait until the end of the week when she got her '$40 a week spending money allowance' (Marilyn's financial arrangement with her business partner Milton Greene, who otherwise covered rent, groceries, etc.), and she would reimburse him. This is not a Marilyn that many people know about.

I also recall that on that June 7th, Marilyn went to see Gwen Verdon in the Broadway stage production of *Damn Yankees* at the 46th Street Theatre. Having already taken pictures of her departing the Waldorf Towers, I then actually beat her car to the theatre on foot! I have pictures of her on East 50th Street, and I have another of her taken short minutes later getting out of a car at the theatre on the West Side of town.

Then there was the night when she came out of the Towers with an escort, her Cadillac parked on Park Avenue at 50th Street, facing in the uptown direction. The Monroe Six and I were about, and maybe a little shy because she was with this guy. In any event, they got into her car and the convertible top had been down until she pushed the mechanism to make the top go up. While the top was going up, one of the Six hailed a taxicab, and all the cab driver knew in the next seconds was that both passenger doors of his cab flew open and all at once seven people fell into the back, onto the seat and on the floor in a pile, a pile of people all ordering him to 'Follow that car! That's Marilyn Monroe!' Our quest had been to get into the taxicab while the Caddy roof was going up so that she wouldn't see us doing this. We wanted to be invisible.

The cab driver got very excited because it was Marilyn Monroe. She was heading for a restaurant called Chez Vito. We drove up Park Avenue, her Cadillac leading the taxi, and when her car rounded the curve of the island in the middle of the avenue and came to a pause at the red light, waiting to go westward on the street where the restaurant was, our cab driver couldn't help himself, he pulled up alongside her; he had to see her! At that point, Marilyn looked over at what should have been an empty taxicab with only a cab driver inside and she leaned out of her car and peering into our back seat, said, 'What are you all doing down there?' to this pile of familiar bodies. It was extremely embarrassing to one and all, a moment to forget until that future time when it could be looked back upon and laughed at.

That July I took my eight-year-old sister Cathy to see Monroe on the big screen in *The Seven Year Itch*, then took

A 'method' actress departs from the Actors Studio, incognito, after her lesson with Strasberg. She took her art seriously and always worked hard to improve her acting.

On the way to see the Broadway play *Inherit the Wind* at the National Theatre on West 41st Street, July 27th, 1955. Dressed simply in a white suit and orange scarf, showing off her tan, she looked fabulous that night.

Cathy over to the Waldorf to meet Marilyn in person, a happening both ladies seemed to enjoy a lot. On the 23rd of the month, once again in the Waldorf garage, I took some colour photographs of Marilyn which are simply sensational. Her face free of make-up, she is wearing sunglasses, and is bound for the Ocean Beach section of Fire Island to weekend with the Strasbergs there. Subsequently, when her Cadillac pulled out of 50th Street to turn onto Lexington Avenue, I shouted to her and Marilyn turned around, her hands firmly clasped to the steering wheel in front of her, and I took a photograph of her in which she is just another part of a vista of images; a Loew's movie theatre, a Mayflower Coffee Shop, the automobile she is sitting in. For some reason never articulated to me, this became for a time her favourite photograph. She asked me for it and finally I loaned her the original colour slide. We then argued for weeks until I got it back. Of course, this led me to wonder just why she favoured this one picture? The only answer I could come up with was that the camera lens was for once not 'right up her nose', as it were. She is just a normal element in a normal setting in this photo-image. I think that is why she liked this particular picture so much, because it defined her as a very real person.

Incidentally, she then took off and drove downtown on Lexington Avenue in a manner I can only refer to as that of a 'California driver'. Lexington Avenue was then a two-lane, two-way traffic thoroughfare. Monroe actually pulled out into the opposing lane to go around the other cars directly in front of her vehicle. Watching helplessly as Marilyn drove towards oncoming cars was no easy moment for me; as they say, 'my heart was in my mouth'! Also, having been raised in California, Marilyn had what I called a 'West Coast mentality'. In New York City, you go to 'the East Side', 'the West Side', 'uptown', 'downtown'. Whenever Marilyn would hail a taxicab, the driver might inquire, 'Which way are you going?', and she would respond, 'I'm going that way', pointing her finger in the direction towards which she was heading. She would never say 'East, West, uptown, downtown'.

On July 27th, Marilyn went to the National Theatre on West 41st Street to see a play, *Inherit the Wind*. Her 'look' that night remains memorable. Monroe was out amongst the public, attending the theatre, and the only make-up on her face was a very minute touch of orange-coloured lipstick. She had on a white suit cut with a deep V in front, an orange scarf around her neck, white high heels, and a great summer tan. She looked quite simply out of this world!

As to Marilyn's real world at that time, allow me to describe what I found beyond the door to Suite 2728 in the Waldorf Towers. In the small apartment, there was a living room, a bedroom, a bath, and a kitchen. You entered Marilyn's apartment directly into the living room, and on a bulletin board there on the right-hand wall (bulletin boards reveal much about we who use them) were items that stay even today in my memory. Pages from foreign magazines; a picture of Albert Einstein, of his face; and another picture of Einstein walking down a road, seen from behind. There was another page that appeared to me to be a picture of a cluster of hungry orphans all huddled together. Sitting on a little table on the left side of the room was a sketch of Marilyn that was quite wonderful, just a few simple lines composing her face – almost a caricature, but very beautiful – and it was executed by actor Zero Mostel, signed by Mostel, who in private life was a friend of Marilyn's.

If as you went into the apartment you veered to your left, you entered the kitchen, which was as dull an example of a kitchen as I've ever seen. Indeed, the most memorable item in the room was the refrigerator. I am exaggerating, of course, but there seemed to be about a thousand jars on top of her refrigerator of hormone creams and so on, mixtures of every kind. And I knew for sure that whatever it was that she put on her face to maintain that flawless skin was sitting there in front of me on top of that otherwise nondescript refrigerator!

The bedroom was directly to the right as you entered the apartment. Marilyn's bed was against the wall that bordered the living room, and hung over her bed was this enormous painting of Abraham Lincoln. Even though I'd read about the painting being there, somehow nothing prepared me for the actual sight of it! On a more personal note, I noticed that Marilyn's telephone was turned into the bed's headboard, so that her private number was not readily obvious to just anyone who might be passing through to use her bathroom. Speaking of Marilyn's private telephone numbers, for a period of time several years earlier, Monroe affixed a bogus number to her telephone dial, and when those who lifted that number dialed same they reached the City Morgue! Meanwhile, back in Marilyn's bedroom, her shoes, most of them Italian-made (very elegant, the high heels in particular) were all nestled on the floor of the closet at the foot of the bed. To the left of that closet was her bathroom, in which there were gold fixtures on the sink. I had never seen gold fixtures before, so I was very much impressed by this. There were also, in the bedroom and back in the living room, private recordings made by Marilyn of songs like *Love Me or Leave Me*, and these personal recordings of hers were strewn casually about on the floor near the windows that overlooked the East River. These discs, recorded in that era's 78 rpm mode, were just lying about with plain home-typed labels on them reading 'Marilyn Monroe', then the title of the song she had sung that was imprisoned on the disc. I quickly developed an incredible temptation to 'borrow' one of the discs, but didn't allow myself to do it. It was during this time that Marilyn did an improvisation at the Actors Studio in which she sang 'a song called *Like a Rolling Stone*'.

When Marilyn flew to Bement, Illinois that summer to participate in an Abraham Lincoln Centennial, she spoofed her own 'dumb blonde' screen image by carrying a large book and publicly flaunting its cover, which read *Lincoln: A Picture Story of his Life*. Now, the lady could read, but the book Marilyn held in her hands for all the world to see was a picture book! The Monroe Six and I went to the airport to see Marilyn off, and I remember seeing her new photographer friend Eve Arnold there, too, along with the usual melange of media photographers and reporters. Pete Leonardi had cut and styled Marilyn's hair for the event, giving her something called a 'feather cut', and it looked sensational on her, as my own colour pictures from that day recall. Pete then offered me a newly trimmed lock of Marilyn's platinum hair; these days that very unique piece of genuine Marilyn resides securely in my safe deposit box.

During this very period the Monroe Six and the Haspiel One were not the only people waiting for Marilyn. Easily the most curious personage standing out there on street corners and lurking in dimly lit doorways was none other than Monroe's recent ex, Joe DiMaggio himself! Yes, on a number of evenings I observed Joe as he secretly watched Marilyn's comings and goings. Yet another DiMaggio-Haspiel moment occurred around this time. One night I was walking along West 52nd Street with a friend of mine, Eddie Sullivan (Eddie's sister Rosie being one of my girlfriends), and it happened by chance that Joe DiMaggio was walking directly in front of us, heading for a restaurant he frequented, Toots Shor's. I alerted Eddie, 'That's Joe DiMaggio.' Disbelieving the very possibility, Eddie retorted, 'No, that can't be Joe DiMaggio!' As I've noted before, I never collected autographs, but I happened to have in my pants pocket a colour snapshot that I'd taken of Marilyn back at Frank Delaney's house on January 7th, so I caught up with Joe and requested, 'Excuse me, Mr DiMaggio, can I get you to put your signature on this?', handing him my candid snapshot of his former wife. (Totally out of character for me, but . . .) Joe then looked at the image of Marilyn nestled in his hand, made some by now long-forgotten comment, flipped the snapshot over and put his signature on the back. Handing the picture back to me, DiMaggio then went on into the restaurant. I turned and gave the signed snapshot to Eddie Sullivan, asking him, 'There, now do you believe me?' As to

Spoofing her dumb blonde image, Marilyn holds a book, *Lincoln: A Picture Story of His Life*, on her way to an Abraham Lincoln Centennial in Illinois. She greatly admired Lincoln and had an enormous painting of him above her bed.

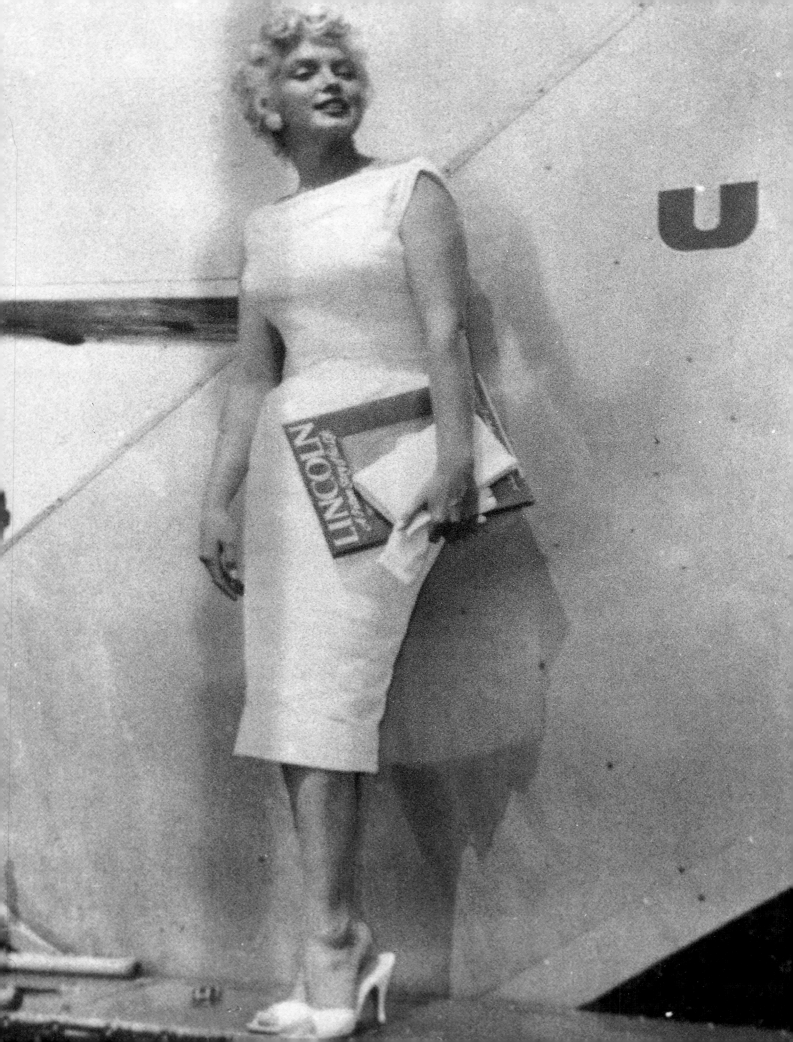

DiMaggio, it was best for everyone concerned that Joe wasn't anywhere nearby the next time I saw his beloved Marilyn in the flesh.

Back then there was a wealthy businessman named Henry Rosenfeld who knew Monroe. One sunny day I witnessed Henry and Marilyn in the midst of a personal encounter that was quite disturbing to me at the time. Marilyn was standing in the outer doorway to the Waldorf Towers, in the middle of the afternoon, wearing a greyish dress that had the look of a simple house dress, Rosenfeld standing in front of her in his eternally tired-looking dark blue suit, white shirt, and red tie (red ties seemed to be Rosenfeld's 'signature'), and Henry was very casually reaching over and stroking Marilyn's buttocks! What disturbed me more than the actions themselves was that she would just stand there and allow this to happen so publicly, because even though I was the sole witness to this moment, anybody else could be passing by. It seemed to me that it was wrong, publicly at least; and especially so given the morals of the time. The gestures were too obviously intimate as far as I was concerned, and while I can offer no opinion as to just how intimate she may or may not have been with Henry Rosenfeld, it bothered me that she would stand there in so public a setting while Henry transmitted his feelings in Braille! Rosenfeld was a genuinely good friend of Monroe's, I'm certain of this, but his actions didn't strike me as being fatherly. The atmosphere was charged with sexual overtones, obviously, and it seemed clear that Marilyn was bent on standing in that doorway until Rosenfeld took his leave and she could return to Suite 2728 solo. Certainly by now Monroe had accumulated vast experience in how to handle that inevitable situation involving the overly aroused male.

Being an everyday witness to Marilyn's life in progress had sometimes fascinating residual effects. Such as, the platonically speaking very important man-of-the-moment in Marilyn's world, who was by all immediate accounts a bisexual individual, married, a father, and ever about with his constantly present male companion. One evening the 'knowing' wife in this triangle got even, right in front of my eyes – unbeknown to her and him – when she proceeded to make love with her husband's lover in the back seat of an automobile while her husband was busy visiting with Marilyn in her Waldorf Towers suite. As I look back on those days I remember that the wife in question was rarely about, that the two men (both of them now deceased) were almost inseparable. Almost. There was a subsequent evening when the husband came on to me in a very suggestive way inside Marilyn's Sutton Place apartment. Marilyn herself seemed oblivious to his overt actions towards me, and while proximity to Monroe would from time to time afford me various full-blown sexual encounters with several of her 'people', both famous and otherwise, this was an invitation that I chose to ignore. Besides, with luscious Marilyn right there in front of me, no known entity on earth could have taken my attention away.

Bringing the subject of sex back to Marilyn, it was around this time that a sensational revelation concerning Monroe's past seems to have made its way into the future cornucopia of Marilyn mythology. Amy Greene was directly responsible for initiating

the tale that Monroe gave birth as a teenager to a baby that she then gave up for adoption. I don't believe for even a moment that Norma Jeane/Marilyn actually had that baby, but I think I can surmise whence the story first emerged. Amy and Milton Greene had a small child, a son named Josh, and during this period of time in which Amy's husband was fully occupied tending to the affairs of Marilyn Monroe, which must have given Mrs Greene not a small amount of social grief among their peers, not to omit the public in general, the one certain thing that a potentially jealous Amy had to throw in the childless

'Hi, Jimmy!' A smiling greeting for me in this picture taken on Park Avenue in summer, 1955.

Marilyn's face was the baby Amy had had with Milton, babies being the ultimate female achievement. I have the distinct feeling that one day the method actress in Marilyn overtook reality and rose to the occasion by giving an Academy Award performance for Amy about 'the baby' she had had. Most plausibly this is the real origin of that particular Monroe legend.

Further illumination on the subject demands that I comment on the fact that former Monroe maid and author Lena (*Marilyn Monroe Confidential*) Pepitone also laid claim to having been told such a tale by her employer around 1957–8. I simply cannot take Pepitone quotes attributed to Monroe very seriously, since even today Lena requires an interpreter when confronting the English language, herself relying almost completely on the Italian language as a means of communication. And in April of 1990 the Marilyn and Baby myth was enlarged upon once again, this time by author Ted (*Norma Jean: A Hollywood Love Story*) Jordan's tease announcement that his second Monroe book would advise the world that '. . . in the late 1940s in the back of a Santa Monica drugstore called Doc Law's', Monroe gave birth to 'either' his or his uncle's 'daughter'. I don't doubt Jordan's confusion in this matter, in as much as a picture published by Jordan as that of 'Norma Jean with my uncle, Ted Lewis' turns out actually to be a photograph of Monroe with her 1954 divorce attorney, Jerry Giesler! Additionally, in the European edition of his initial Monroe effort Jordan also served up 'my amateur photograph' of Norma Jeane – an image that I, James Robert Haspiel, reproduced back in 1975 from a 16-mm model agency film test of Norma Jeane shot around 1945; my own identifying 'JRH' initials even appear in the print of the picture published in this version of the Ted Jordan book! Also in the European edition, there is a full-page nude picture – 'An intimate shot, the one I treasure most. Norma Jean's beauty still staggers me' – that is in absolute fact a picture of a very minor pinup model/actress of the 1950s named Arline Hunter. To state flatly that Ted Jordan's credibility is suspect is to be more than generous with this Monroe biographer. It should be noted that by the time it reached American shores under its new title, *Norma Jean: My Secret Life with*

A studio shot taken in 1952, during the period when Marilyn was filming *Niagara*.

Above: At the party that announced the launch of Marilyn Monroe Productions, on January 7th, 1955. In fact, the only film that the company ever produced was *The Prince and the Showgirl*, which was released in 1957.

Left: One of Marilyn's fan club presidents, Nathan Puckett, looks on from the background during a visit to New York to see Marilyn in June 1955.

Opposite: A profile captured by me in January 1955.

Above: Of all the pictures I took of Marilyn, this was her favourite – I think because she blends so naturally into the New York City landscape.

Right: Marilyn, without her Monroe persona, could regularly walk down busy New York streets unrecognized.

Opposite: The first picture of Marilyn and I together, taken at her hotel on September 12th, 1954, days after she arrived in New York to film *The Seven Year Itch*.

Opposite: Departing from New York for Hollywood to film *Bus Stop*.

Marilyn with Arthur Miller about to board a plane in July 1958, once again for Hollywood, where this time she will film *Some Like It Hot*.

Above: Out for a walk, wearing a favourite 'teddy bear' coat.

Opposite: A pensive moment on the set of *Some Like It Hot.*

Opposite: At the post–premiere party for *Some Like It Hot.*

Above: The best present of all, a twenty-first birthday kiss from Marilyn.

After the costume tests for
The Misfits on July 8th,
1960, to which the Monroe
Six and I were invited.

Opposite: My most valued
picture of Marilyn –
standing alone at the corner
of 93rd Street and Lexington
Avenue in February 1956.

Marilyn's final screen minutes are caught on film for *Something's Got to Give*, taken on her thirty-sixth birthday – June 1st, 1962.

Opposite: A delighted Marilyn attends Yves Montand's one-man-show on Broadway, 1959.

Marilyn Monroe, the picture section of Jordan's book had undergone some very question-able but obvious surgery. All of the photo-images noted above had been conveniently deleted from same for the American public's consumption.

If Jordan could not distinguish his own uncle from attorney Giesler, possibly he couldn't distinguish a young Arline Hunter from the youthful Norma Jeane; perhaps in real life as in 'reel life' Ms Hunter is in fact the 'Norma Jean' of Jordan's tales?

Having raised the spectre of Miss Arline Hunter, allow me to educate those among you out there who may have viewed with a certain fascination an infamous nudie film short called *The Apple-Knockers and the Coke* starring 'Marilyn Monroe'. Sorry, folks, but that wasn't really Marilyn up there on your silver screens or, courtesy of the medium of videotape, over there on your TV screens. The real story behind this 'reel story' goes as follows —

MARILYN MONROE AND THE BLUE MOVIE

The photographer adjusted his camera, and peering through its viewfinder, centred his lens on the beautiful model lying completely naked on a flame-red cloth throw beneath him. They were working for a certain effect and the desired pose began to find its form as the model stretched her nude torso into a full-length profile, carefully arching her left leg until its foot rested just below the knee of her right leg. Now she stretched her left arm upwards and away from her and folded her right arm into a near perfect recreation of a nude calendar pose of several years before entitled 'A New Wrinkle – originally posed for by a then little-known starlet named Marilyn Monroe. This newest version of the pose would become *Playboy* magazine's centrefold of August 1954, and its current model, Arline Hunter, would achieve a small measure of fame in 'girlie' magazines of the mid-1950s as a 'Marilyn Monroe lookalike'.

Enroute to Madison Square
Garden to sing *Happy
Birthday* to President
Kennedy on May 19th, 1962.

Early on, Arline Hunter discovered that she could make money posing as Monroe in 'quickie 16-mm stag-reel nudie films', and to update the image she had her then long tresses cut and fashioned in the Monroe hairstyle of 1952. Stag-film buffs could soon purchase what were represented as 'movies of the young Marilyn in the nude', titles such as *Hollywood Honey* and *Blonde Temptress* among them. As a visual sit-in of the fabled Monroe image, Miss Hunter could be glimpsed in big screen feature films, as well.

Some sixteen years after Hunter's Monroe-styled appearance in *Playboy*, in December 1970 a predominantly male audience at a movie theatre on New York City's Great White Way focused keen eyes upon the screen as they read the credits of a movie-within-a-movie: 'High-Quality films presents Marilyn Monroe in *The Apple-Knockers and the Coke*'. The theatre marquee outside the darkened auditorium advertised '*Hollywood Blue . . .* Private authentic films of the stars. Unbelievable!' Yes, 'unbelievable'! Elsewhere, Marilyn's nudie double, now in her forties, went about the business of everyday living, perhaps unaware that this film she had made almost twenty years before was now being shown as part of this stag-movies retrospective. Ultimately, Hunter's Monroe masquerade in that nudie short resulted in a box office bonanza for those theatres daring enough to utilize the Monroe name and image in their advertisements. Miss Hunter's initial big screen appearance of any length was in a now lost feature film entitled *A Virgin in Hollywood*. Cameo-wise, Arline Hunter's film credits include: *Revolt in the Big House* (Allied Artists/1959); *Sex Kittens Go to College* (Allied Artists/1960); *Madison Avenue* (Twentieth Century-Fox/1962); and *Don't Worry, We'll Think of a Title* (United Artists/1966).

Leaving this 'reel Marilyn' behind and returning to the real Marilyn, in explaining her avoidance of the sun, Monroe once said, 'I like to feel blonde all over.' Well then, who was this bronzed goddess standing before my lens wearing a trenchcoat over an orange pullover shirt-blouse and chomping on popcorn supplied by one of the Monroe

Marilyn holding bogus pornographic letters and snapshots of a Monroe lookalike, appears in a California courtroom in 1952 to put a stop to the mail order business being promoted at her professional expense.

Six? Another of my personal photographs shows that same bronzed Marilyn arriving at the Anta Theatre on Broadway to attend a performance of *The Skin of Our Teeth*. Perhaps 1955 was her 'Year of the Tan'. In any event, on one September evening Marilyn returned to the Towers from an unhappy weekend spent at Fire Island in the company of a producer. I believe they had stayed at the Ocean Beach cottage of Lee and Paula Strasberg. I don't recall who told me, but 'Monroe couldn't stand this guy!', yet somehow she had had to spend the weekend in his company. On that 'date' from which she returned, I'll call it a date for lack of a better word, she was wearing a black woollen coat, a garment destined to leave me with a vivid, lifelong memory.

At some point the Strasberg family moved from West 86th Street down to 135 Central Park West, between 73rd and 74th Streets. It was there that Monroe would now continue her visits, her acting lessons with Lee, and often she would walk home from that location to East 50th Street, to the Waldorf Towers. One evening she trekked those twenty-eight blocks in the rain, and she was wearing that same woollen coat. By the time she arrived home, the coat was dragging along the glistening cement sidewalk, under the weight of the water soaked wool; and Marilyn was all but drenched through to her alabaster-turned-bronze skin, the back of her woollen coat looking not unlike the train of an ominous black wedding dress.

It was during those same walks that she did something that used to get me somewhat angry. Passersby would stop her along Central Park West and exclaim, 'Oh, you're Marilyn Monroe!', and she

On this night in September 1955, I met Marilyn when she had just returned from an unhappy weekend.

Marilyn would sometimes walk back home from her private acting lessons with Lee Strasberg. It was on one such night that heavy rain drenched her black woollen coat, seen in this picture.

would respond, 'No, I'm not, I'm Mamie Van Doren,' or, 'No, I'm Sheree North,' because she knew this would diminish their original interest. Both Van Doren and North were currently being lauded as 'new' Marilyns. I used to admonish Marilyn, 'How can you say that? Don't you realize that these people will go around for the rest of their lives saying, "I saw Mamie Van Doren in person and she's got Marilyn Monroe beat by a mile!"' Years later I related this story to Sheree North in my kitchen one evening, her response being a healthy chuckle at the thought of Monroe claiming to be her.

In what seemed like a world of cinema blondes, there was also a movie brunette around. While Marilyn was still living at the Waldorf, her former co-star Jane Russell (*Gentlemen Prefer Blondes*) was staying at a hotel located a couple of blocks away. I remember that we – the Six and I – had to deliver a note from Monroe to Russell. I don't recall anything else about the moment, other than that we did so as requested by our 'Mazzie'.

Then came the incident that was to be the catalyst of an event that would ultimately produce my memory-of-memories. As I was approaching the Towers one day in mid-afternoon, Marilyn was just walking out of the doorway, and I found myself looking directly at what can only be described as a 'schoolmarm'. She was wearing a high-necked, long-sleeved, grey wool dress and cuban heels, she had on some light make-up, and her hair was upswept into a tiny golden chignon. This was a Marilyn I had not seen before! I didn't know where her appointment was, or with whom, who she was supposed to impress or in what way, but she was incredibly elegant, and in fact, quite severe-looking. Suppressing my amazement, I called, 'Marilyn', and she answered, 'I'm in a hurry, Jimmy, I can't stop.' As she was getting into a waiting limo, I shot back, 'Oh, for Christ's sake, you never pay any attention to me!', and stormed off in a huff, deciding that next time around I was going to snub her.

Well, realistically speaking, the only way for me to ignore Marilyn was actually to go to her; she wasn't going to come to my stoop so I had to go to hers. There was no other way. In order to achieve my intentioned goal, a day or so later I sat myself down on a stoop located directly across from the entrance to the Waldorf Towers. There was a church there, and this stoop was at the side of the church. (Sometime later I got arrested on that very same stoop, but 'later'; it's a very funny story.) Alright, so I was firmly implanted on the stoop across from the doorway I expected Marilyn to emerge from or arrive at, fully intending to ignore her (given the right inspiration the mind can work wonders!), when suddenly I looked up in the afternoon sunshine and spotted the familiar red Ford convertible pulling into the island area on Park Avenue at 50th Street. It was pointed towards the Towers' entrance, motionless, waiting for the red light to turn green. Peter was at the wheel and Marilyn was sitting next to him in the passenger seat in front. I could see from where I was sitting that she had make-up on, and was wearing a V-necked white sweater (she was also decked out in a form-fitting black skirt and black high heels).

The light changed and the car started up, and the next thing I knew, Marilyn slid up onto the back of her seat, as a person would riding in an open car in a parade, and she started to wave her arms enthusiastically in my direction. Suddenly she was shouting, 'Jimmy! Jimmy!', and I nearly went into cardiac arrest! I had come here to ignore her, yet my eyes were as wide open as could be, with my mouth running a close second. The car pulled down into the street, and the whole time Marilyn was waving and yelling out my name. Peter brought the vehicle to a stop directly across from me, and she was sitting there on the back of her seat still yelling and carrying on, and everybody passing by had just stopped dead in their tracks. Finally, catching my breath, I rose up off the stoop and ran across the street, and as I was coming around the back of the car, Marilyn slid down into her seat, all the way down. She was looking back towards me, and I remember that the bright sunlight illuminated the rich blue in her eyes. As I arrived at her side she looked up at me, and in an intentional whisper, she asked, 'Did I pay enough attention to you today, Jimmy?' Obviously my lament from our previous encounter had registered strongly with her.

I said I was arrested on that church stoop, which is true. I was sitting there one afternoon, at the age of seventeen, when a policeman came along. Now, it should be noted that the stoop in question was not an in-use entrance to anything at that time. There was a gate at the top of its stairs that was permanently locked. Of course, given Marilyn's comings and goings, I was a fairly familiar person in the area by now. Anyway, this policeman came along while I was sitting there basking in the sunshine, and he tapped me on my knee with his night stick and ordered me to 'Beat it!' I told him, 'Officer, I sit here everyday,' and pointing towards the Waldorf Towers across the street, I continued, 'You can even ask the doorman over there; he knows me.' The cop then asked, 'Are you through?' and I answered, 'Yes.' He then repeated his 'Beat it!' edict with additional emphasis, and I stood up and, with considerable anger, said, 'What the fuck would you like me to do? Go rob a car?' Stepping off the stoop, I added, 'You bastard!' As I continued by him he put a firm hand on my shoulder and I swung around and landed a heavy-duty punch right in his face. Now, you *don't* punch a uniformed cop. For so doing, I found myself imprisoned in the Tombs jailhouse overnight. Next morning I found myself in court, facing a female judge who, having listened intently to my 'waiting for Marilyn' story, advised me, 'I'm going to let you go, but I want you to understand that there are more women in this world besides Marilyn Monroe.' End of story.

CLOSER
ENCOUNTERS

Encounters with Marilyn were not always the result of pursuit. As I was walking along Park Avenue one afternoon, I remember that I was sort of looking downwards and suddenly I heard some very familiar laughter coming in my direction. The first thing my eyes lit upon were these alabaster-toned ankles encased in black flat shoes, and my gaze then travelled upwards along the cloth of her also familiar beige polo coat. This encounter happened during the period when Marilyn was preparing to move out of her sublet at the Waldorf Towers and over to 2 Sutton Place, at 57th Street and the East River, to an apartment there, 8E on the eighth floor. That was in the fall of 1955.

There is a wonderful memory from that period. I was out walking on a Sunday morning in her area, but I wasn't expecting to see Marilyn at that hour of the day. I was just walking in her neighbourhood simply because it was such a beautiful neighbourhood, and as I was walking along Sutton Place South I naturally looked up at her windows, and there she was! She was wearing a baby blue terry-cloth bathrobe, leaning on her windowsill, and looking out in the early morning sunshine towards the East River. She had to look across diagonally because there was an apartment building opposite blocking any direct view. I just leaned on the corner of that building opposite her and watched her for awhile, while she watched the boats cruising along the East River, the birds flying about, and the spectacle of a magnificent city awakening to a new day. Finally, she scanned the street below and noticed me looking up at her, at which point we exchanged silent greetings with gestures, from which Marilyn's smile lingers to this very day.

As on the earlier evening of the premiere of *East of Eden*, there was another time when she was unspeakably beautiful, just unspeakably. By now, Marilyn had bought herself a black Ford Thunderbird convertible car. On this particular day, she emerged from 2 Sutton Place wearing a grey kerchief, grey blouse, grey skirt with matching belt, grey high heels, entirely co-ordinated, and she had on light pink lipstick. Marilyn

A model, passing herself off as Marilyn in nude pictures, is proved in court to be an imposter when the snapshots held by the real Marilyn in this picture show a birthmark clearly absent from Marilyn's skin.

THE ULTIMATE LOOK AT THE LEGEND

was going someplace alone in her T-bird car. In fact, the sole reason I recollect this encounter is because of the incredible look of her. These two moments, the very public *East of Eden* premiere, and the very private 'Lady-Grey' day, placed a Marilyn before my eyes who could not be described by any combination of words in a dictionary; she was just that breathtakingly gorgeous, that memorable. It has since been suggested that on the day Marilyn first went to meet her future mother-in-law, Augusta Miller, she was dressed all in grey.

Memorable. On the other hand, from the period of eight years that produced my memories of Marilyn, any number of our encounters have taken their natural leave from my powers of recollection. For example, on October 5th, 1955, Monroe attended the Broadway opening of *The Diary of Anne Frank*, as well as joining its star, Susan Strasberg, at Sardi's Restaurant on West 44th Street following the play. In a subsequent issue of *Life* magazine, there was published a picture of Marilyn in which I am standing directly next to her. I don't remember this particular evening at all, yet there exists this picture that demonstrates quite clearly that I was there too. Ergo, how many other meetings must have occurred without even any photographs to jog my personal memories of them.

Jayne Mansfield stops by her idol at a post-screening party at the Astor Hotel in December 1955. Jayne tried to emulate Marilyn in every way, but she was never to experience the same success and adulation that Marilyn knew.

From the forgotten to the unforgettable: that December 12th, a film called *The Rose Tattoo* premiered at the Astor Theatre, with a post-screening party held at the Astor Hotel. The premiere and the party were both attended by Monroe, and that was the night that a fascinated Jayne Mansfield wiggled up to Marilyn's table and there were some rare photo-images captured of the legendary one and her soon-to-be cinematic shadow. Mansfield adored Monroe, as was made all too obvious by her public emulations of Marilyn.

The in-person and celluloid Jayne Mansfields were never to realize anything more than a pale reflection of the object of Mansfield's off-screen worship. While Jayne usually elicited casual smiles from passersby, Monroe was more likely to inspire feelings bordering on awe. And it was this awesome Marilyn Monroe who turned up at the Broadway opening of the new Arthur Miller play, *A View from the Bridge*. I remember walking into the theatre that night, and obviously Monroe was the kind of personage you would expect to find seated fourth row centre. Instead, I think in deference to the author and his work, Marilyn was seated discreetly to the left side of the orchestra, towards the middle of the theatre. I walked down the aisle and just took a quiet look at her; she was once again incredible-looking on this night, Thursday, September 29th, 1955, at the Coronet Theatre.

Despite the fact that I obviously adored Marilyn, I was yet capable of expressing anger with her. Over the previous months I had gotten used to being invited into taxicabs with Marilyn, I should say *by* Marilyn, and on this particular day, at the precise time that I knew she would be leaving for a certain destination, I arrived at 2 Sutton Place. Her cab was in place in the alcove there; she had just got into it, and I simply opened the other door and invited myself in. She looked over at me and said with a gentle firmness, 'No, Jimmy, I need to be alone right now.' Immediately, she opened her wallet, and there was a lot of 'green' in it, and she started to pull up a $20 bill, suggesting that I take my own cab to 'our' destination. I became at once offended and promptly slammed the cab door in her face! I was wrong to behave towards her in this manner, of course, but the act itself was part of the fabric of our relationship and, if examined truthfully, this was the kind of moment that told her quite clearly that I also viewed her as a peer, a human being rather than an object. Slamming the door in her face, or telling her to 'Go to hell!', which I did at some other point, these were moments in which, as negative as they were, Marilyn was beginning to recognize that I was not always keeping her up on a pedestal of some kind, which had to be something that she was very sick of with those people who were around her most of the time.

In the situation in which Marilyn offered me $20 to take my own cab, her own taxi obviously had a destination: 155 East 93rd Street, an apartment building at the corner of Lexington Avenue. I choose to be somewhat discreet about this part of the story. Marilyn visited that building five days a week; two mornings, three afternoons a week, and in a sense our relationship kind of flourished there. It was more of a one-on-one situation; she didn't meet the public there. The Monroe Six were at work during these hours, so it was essentially Marilyn being there for her own personal-but-known-to-me reasons, and I, even though I was employed, could usually arrange to be there to connect up with her. What is notable about this particular area of New York City is that it became what I think of as Marilyn's real world. By that I mean that, rather than at Sutton Place, she would do her grocery shopping there, and so on.

Speaking of groceries, there was a little store there, kind of a mom-and-pop grocery store between 93rd and 94th Streets, on the west side of Lexington Avenue. Marilyn was going to do an improvisation at the Actors Studio, in which she was supposed to 'be a kitten'; they had little kittens in the store, and she borrowed one of them and studied it for a week, watching intently how it moved, behaved, rolled on the floor, its attitude in general. Out of those observations, she presented her improvisation in class as a little kitten.

Marilyn Monroe had grown used to being the object of great attention, the recipient of immediate consumer service, if you will, thus the next recollection might at the very least amuse the reader. Between 92nd and 93rd Streets, on the west side of Lexington Avenue, was a small luncheonette called Andros Food Shop. One morning when Marilyn emerged from her appointment, she walked into Andros and sat down at the counter there. She was wearing her sunglasses, so the world was, shall we say, a little darker, particularly indoors, for her. So there she was, seated at the counter waiting for service, and I was across the street watching her, and a couple of men were coming into the place with bags of ice cubes, with bread and rolls, and assorted other deliveries. What Marilyn hadn't realized was that the luncheonette hadn't really opened yet. Andros' door was opened for the delivery men who were coming and going, and she was just sitting there, being fairly impatient, waiting to be served, but there wasn't going to be any service for at least half-an-hour! One can only imagine how differently the story would have played had those delivery men realized that the restless customer, our Norma Jeane of yesteryear, was their movie goddess, 'Marilyn Monroe'!

Finally, she emerged from Andros Food Shop, we greeted, Marilyn hailed a taxicab and beckoned me into it, and we were off. During one of those memorable cab rides, I remember once bringing up the subject of *Love Happy*, a film in which she had played what we now call a 'cameo' role during her starlet days, and suddenly Marilyn burst into gales of laughter as she fell back into the corner of the cab, laughing her head off over 'Lester Cowan, the producer'. Given the legion of tales by now floating about regarding producers-vs-starlets, including the infamous one about Monroe's own sexual rejection of Columbia Pictures boss Harry Cohn, as well as comedian Groucho Marx's own stories of his enthusiastic but failed attempts to seduce Monroe during the filming of *Love Happy*, I couldn't muster up the nerve to ask her why she was so gleefully holding her hand over her mouth and laughing like a little girl who had managed somehow to outwit the big bad wolf. Thus we don't know the actual finale of this retrospective memory of Monroe's.

From the ridiculous to the sublime (for me, at least), now comes a very pivotal moment. We were riding in yet another taxicab, and she was expressing herself on some now forgotten subject, then Marilyn said, ' . . . but, Jimmy . . . '; and a sentence later a light bulb went on in my head, and I asked, 'Wait a minute. What did you just say?' Now, this kind of moment could have happened to any one of you out there. Say you have just walked into a room, and for instance, Barbra Streisand is there; now, whether you're interested in her or not, you already know much about her, because she is such a highly publicized personage. Meanwhile, this woman doesn't know anything at all about you. Originally, I had walked up to 'Marilyn Monroe' already knowing nearly her entire history, yet she didn't know a single thing about me. And despite every one of the previous times that she had addressed me as 'Jimmy', it had never before occurred to me that I had never actually introduced myself to her! Now, this is a long time and many personal encounters later, and for some reason still unknown to me, this time, when I heard her say 'Jimmy' a bell went off in my head. When I asked, 'What did you just say?', Marilyn immediately began to repeat her just-expressed thought, and I interrupted her with, 'No, no,' asking, 'What did you call me?' As she sat there staring at me, somewhat wide-eyed, Marilyn responded, 'I called you "Jimmy"; your name is James Robert Haspiel,' then spelling out with a pointed emphasis, 'H-A-S-P-I-E-L'. End of quote. What had happened was that earlier Marilyn had approached a member of the Monroe Six to inquire about me, where I came from, etcetera, because I was so preoccupied with her that I hadn't volunteered any informa-tion as to exactly who I was.

Who was I? I had entered this universe at the Bushwick Hospital in Brooklyn, New York, on February 21st in the year 1938. That very week my mother left my father, the man she had married three years before, and in doing so, she set off a chain of events that were destined to make almost painfully obvious, certain similarities between my early years and those of the child called Norma Jeane. As it had been in her life, so it was true of mine, that I was 'farmed out', as it were, living my first seven years in other people's homes; people usually bent on treating 'the outsider' as such, therefore effectively denying me, and before me, Norma Jeane, any foundation that might give us any real sense of belonging. Ultimately, I had experienced a rather tragic childhood, so there was more than likely some sort of identification with Monroe happening there. For me and Marilyn, the old expression 'One wolf recognizes another' would be modified to read, 'One waif recognizes . . . '.

Early traumas: in addition to an incident that took place in 1946, in which I watched helplessly as my first little 'girlfriend' perished in an apartment blaze in the small hours of the morning, and another moment in which I looked on as a newborn infant's severed head was retrieved from a local garbage can, the drama of my early youth also included suicide attempts before my child's eyes by both my mother and a stepsister, as well as ever-increasing physical violence visited upon my body (I once had the thousand-needles of a wire hairbrush slammed firmly into the top of my scalp; I was eight years old at the time!). These events occurred from around 1945 through 1954, at which point I finally fled from my 'home' to live, if briefly, on the streets and roofs of the city. I was fifteen years old. Educationally, I never got past the first year of high school, and didn't go to college.

You could say rather easily that the teenaged Jimmy and the girl they called Norma Jeane both knew only too well about the struggle to survive intact in what back then seemed an alien world of educated people living in well-grounded family structures, both emotionally and materially speaking. It was a world in which I often found for myself enough solace in the affordable cake of soap that kept me at least clean, to also keep me going forward.

But as far as one might go, the original pain remained, and so I always felt that special bonding with Marilyn that all 'displaced' persons might inevitably experience with one another. But as we would both eventually know, survival can be achieved.

Suffice it to say that there are not a few people in my life today who marvel that I never turned to alcohol and/or drugs. Never. But enough self-retrospection. In any event, in 1955, my friends the Monroe Six were a more than respectable lot of individuals, all gainfully employed.

The ultimate of all Marilyn Monroe collectors yet known to me, Frieda Hull, by then in her mid-twenties, had come to the Waldorf Towers from the home she owned in Richmond Hill, New York, which she then shared with the still teenaged Edith Pitts, the former girlfriend of Hull's recently deceased brother. In fact, it was the shared grief over his tragic passing that cemented their lifelong friendship. Also in the house was Hull's Aunt Lizzie, a delight of a person who passed on in the late 1960s. Both Frieda and Edith had caught their first glimpse of Monroe on a movie screen in *The Asphalt Jungle*, their second glimpse on the television screen in Monroe's 1950 commercial for Royal Triton Motor Oil. Impressed, the two subsequently made their way to the St Regis Hotel in 1954 to view Marilyn in person, and now even more impressed, showed up for the New York City filming of Monroe's famed skirt-blowing scene for *The Seven Year Itch*.

To know Frieda Hull was to experience constantly the residual effects of the quickest wit imaginable. Hull had the ability to render you senseless and doubled over in laughter on a regular basis. Actually, her collection of Monroe memorabilia began at the onset of Norma Jeane's career in the 1940s, pre-dating Marilyn's real fame, and thereby giving her memorabilia a unique advantage over most other collections. Hull's other celluloid loves included both June Allyson and Judy Garland, along with a strong attraction to the likes of movie muscleman Steve Reeves. Highly religious, the never-wed Hull to this day remains faithful to the memory of Marilyn ('Mazzie') in her chosen way, which is Frieda's quietude on the subject.

Hull's house-mate, the bespectacled and bubbly Edith Pitts, was a quick-to-laugh brunette with a fondness for the handsome movie males of the day. She once urged me to accept Rock Hudson's 'invitation' to intimacy, 'So you can tell me about it later . . . Go with him, Jimmy!', which I declined. For several years, Edith had a crush on your author, that very feeling bringing us together for dates on a number of occasions throughout the 1950s. A secretary, Pitts subsequently married and moved away with her husband to Arizona, where (sans children) she lives today as . . . a blonde.

The only genuine blonde among the Six, albeit a dark blonde, was the youthful Eileen Collins, who arrived at the Waldorf Towers with her dark-haired and handsome teenaged brother, Jimmy, whose devilish personality and outrageous sense of humour held the power to keep you wide awake into the small hours of the morning during the sometimes long wait for Mazzie. Far more serious than her brother, laughter came less readily to Eileen, but with no less a state of elation. Back then, the Collins kids lived out towards the Rockaways with their family. Sometime around 1955, Jimmy made the pages of *Life* magazine, commenting on Monroe in, of all things, a photo-layout of people typing messages on an Olivetti typewriter then mounted on a pedestal outside their Fifth Avenue store. Olivetti=Monroe; as I've said to many over the years, no matter what the subject, 'Marilyn is like the Golden Blossom Honey: she's in there somewhere!' The last time I saw Jimmy Collins was in the mid-1970s when my wife and I were shopping out near our home in the Hamptons, and I caught a glimpse of him frolicking with some buddies across the store aisle. I have not seen Eileen Collins since 1963.

Not so with John Reilly, my chosen 'brother' in this life. John has been in and out of my life with a certain regularity since January 7th, 1955, when we first met back at that party to announce the formation of Marilyn Monroe Productions. Reilly was yet in his teens on that memorable night, having come down from the Bronx, where he lived with his beloved mother, the recipient of his utter devotion to this very day, even in death. An Irishman, successful professionally, well-travelled, this godfather to my sons, having long ago disposed of his Monroe memorabilia, lives today in Elmhurst,

New York. A man with a generous sense of humour, Reilly remains one of my favourite people on this planet.

Finally, there was the eldest of the actual Six, Gloria Milone, a black-haired, bespectacled woman who resided back then with her older sister, Emma, in Brooklyn, New York. Gloria, having been wrested from her wait outside the Drake Hotel 'to see Ava Gardner', and hustled over 'to see Marilyn Monroe', bringing with her her sharp-edged humour, stayed put at Marilyn's doorway, even subsequently moving out to California just prior to 'Mazzie's' departure for the West Coast from New York City. Today, Milone lives in an apartment interestingly situated just minutes in either direction from the house Marilyn died in and the crypt containing the remains of Monroe.

'The Monroe Six-Plus': there was sometimes a sort of 'mascot' hanging out with the Six, a fifteen-year-old boy named Johnny Duggan. To digress for a moment, Duggan, several members of the Six and myself once slept overnight in friend (and Monroe-competitor) Jayne Mansfield's tiny apartment at New York City's Gorham Hotel, a 1956 happening that set up a potentially scandalous moment for Jayne. Unable to locate her underage son late that night, Duggan's mother had notified the police, who the following day interviewed Mansfield, inquiring as to 'the exact nature' of the youngster's overnight stay. Even after the air had cleared, Jayne worried for weeks that the scandal magazine of the day, *Confidential*, would somehow get hold of the story, distort it ('Jimmy, they'll say we had an orgy!!!'), and that her career would 'be ruined!' *Confidential* missed the story and, ultimately, it would be Jayne's own unwise career choices that would subsequently point her towards professional oblivion.

The Monroe Six and the Haspiel One: Our times together were nothing less than great back in the 1950s, given the combination of Marilyn and rampant humour; I'm fairly certain that if one listens truly hard, the laughter of seven wild and crazy, happy kids still echoes about across from the entrance to the Waldorf Towers on East 50th Street! But laughter aside, around 1955–6, these people of very different lives who called themselves the Monroe Six, deemed that no matter how hard young Jimmy Haspiel tried, he was not to be officially permitted into 'the Club'. In retrospect, I'm actually grateful for that now, but back then it frustrated and hurt me a lot. We all converged on Monroe at about the same time, yet I wasn't allowed 'in'. But in the long run that finally became a positive for me, because it meant that Marilyn didn't relate to me as one of the Six either, that becoming the best part, that I was a separate entity, I was 'James Robert H-A-S-P-I-E-L'. The actuality of it taught me a lifelong lesson about the value of staying original.

Although I was always ready for her, obviously there were times when Monroe was not ready for 'H-A-S-P-I-E-L'. One day, I was walking uptown to meet Marilyn, and as I was crossing Lexington Avenue at 92nd Street, I saw in the American Restaurant, a sort of luncheonette-type restaurant on the corner there, Monroe seated inside at a window table. As I spotted her, she saw me, and at once ducked her head downwards. I say this thing very candidly, because, what does it really matter, you know: that didn't stop me! Anyway, I walked right into the place and went directly to her table and sat myself right down.

Marilyn, fondly nicknamed 'Mazzie' by the Monroe Six, her loyal group of fans, stops to chat with Johnny Duggan – the Six's 'mascot' – on her left.

There was an awkward greeting of some kind between us. There was a magazine out at that time, *Rave* magazine, and Monroe was on their cover, and I think there were thirty-two full pages of Marilyn inside the issue. Subsequently, in a published letter to *Rave*, a reader had referred to Monroe as 'a prostitute'! And I had responded to that with a letter to the magazine, and had a copy of my letter with me on this particular morning. So I showed Marilyn my letter, and I remember she read it, then reached across the table and took my hand in hers, and in a very loving voice, Marilyn said to me, 'Jimmy, you don't have to defend me.' I thought it was very nice of her to say that to me, but I *wanted* to defend her, and here she was caring about me being hurt about these kinds of things being said about her.

The word 'prostitute' evokes yet another memory. I was with Marilyn one sunny afternoon when a female admirer rushed up to her, exclaiming, 'It's Marilyn Monroe! Oh, my God, can I have your autograph?' The woman had a paperback book in her hand, a novel, and usually at the fronts of these publications was a page that had little printing on it, perhaps only one line, and the woman quickly handed Monroe the novel already opened to this nearly vacant page, along with a pen. Monroe took both items into her hands, and looking at the page before her, the pen poised inches above it, suddenly read aloud the single line looming before her eyes: '*How I became a prostitute!*' Wide-eyed, Marilyn announced, 'I can't sign this!', and handed the paperback book back to the woman fan, then signing some other piece of paper, the woman's chequebook, I think, for her.

Again, on the subject of Marilyn Monroe meeting her public, there was an afternoon on East 93rd Street when 'Mazzie' didn't look too well. She was very pasty-looking, wearing a mink coat and high heels, her tousled blonde hair looking really terrible. She had just come out of the building at number 155 and walked up to the corner of Lexington Avenue, and in her obvious state of distraction, she failed to notice me standing on the opposite corner. A city bus pulled up to the corner at which

Monroe was now standing, and with a passenger having instantly recognized her, the remaining people on the bus all came over to one side of the waiting-for-the-green-light vehicle and stared down upon Monroe. I remember feeling troubled, even hurt that these people were seeing her looking this way. Quickly, I walked over to Marilyn and offered, 'Can I get you a taxicab?', and she just as quickly dismissed me. Obviously, she was in an extremely lousy mood, so I turned and took my leave of the area.

The next morning, when we met again, I remember us walking into the Whelan's Drugstore then on the corner of 93rd Street and Lexington Avenue, and I had just handed Marilyn that day's edition of the *New York Times*. Now, it might be relevant to digress here, to let the reader know that at that time one would frequently come upon a column item about Marilyn, such as 'Marilyn Monroe dined at Chez Vito last night' (I'm remembering a specific item naming that particular restaurant, because Marilyn wasn't at Chez Vito; she was with me!). Restaurant managers back then would do that sort of thing, telephone a newspaper columnist and claim, 'Marilyn Monroe was here tonight . . .', that in itself gaining them a valued line in the next day's column, therefore bringing more customers into the establishment. But one would do well to not bring this kind of trivia to Monroe's attention. When in the past I had offered Marilyn a newspaper and said, 'You are in Earl Wilson's column today', her hand went right up between us, her palm facing me, her fingers pointed skywards, and she said, 'No, I'm not interested, Jimmy.' What Marilyn was doing was getting on with her life, as opposed to, say, a Jayne Mansfield, who really cared that she turned up in the gossip columns on a daily basis, no matter what the item, no matter what its tone. By now, Monroe was well beyond that need; she wanted to go and take her acting classes, she didn't want to take time out to consider whatever an Earl Wilson may have said about her today. So I learned early on to bring her the gossip-free *New York Times*, if I brought her a newspaper.

But back to Monroe and her public. On this particular day I had handed Marilyn the *New York Times*, she thanked me, and then she advised, 'I have to make a telephone call, Jimmy.' As we entered the drugstore and stood in line in order for her to get change for the phone, I told her, 'I was very unhappy yesterday afternoon when all those people on the bus saw you looking that way.' Marilyn looked at me and asked: 'Looking what way?', to which I responded, 'Well, Marilyn, you really looked terrible yesterday, and . . .' She had just got the change for the telephone, and she looked over her shoulder and up at me, and with a certain sternness invading her voice, she said 'Well, Jimmy, don't let it bother you!' From the tone of her voice, I realized at once that my comment had impacted strongly on her. Marilyn then walked briskly to the back end of the store, en route passing by a marble soda fountain counter running the length of the place, and she went into a vacant telephone booth. She shut the door (pay phone booths in those days still had doors on them), inserted a coin, and began dialling a number. I could hear her dialling, when suddenly she stopped, the door opened, and the *New York Times* came flying out of the telephone booth, sliding along the length of the marble counter, and came to a full stop just short of falling off the opposite end of the counter, right where I stood. Perfect pitch! You would have thought that Joe DiMaggio had tossed it out of the booth! This incident took place in February of 1956. With the *New York Times* now staring up at me from that counter, I said to myself, 'Oh, my God, Haspiel, you've really done it now!' I didn't pick the newspaper up, I simply walked quietly out of the store – there would be no taxi ride today!

This leads us to the following day. Well, now I was about to test the waters, as it were, because after all, my present thinking was, 'She doesn't like me anymore'. So I went back to 93rd Street because, once again, I had to present myself, she wasn't going to come and find me. I was sitting there in the morning sunshine, actually down on the sidewalk cement, my back resting against the building, when she came out of number

155. The sidewalk itself was on an incline, so she was now walking upwards on it towards me, and it was with some degree of intention that I did not look in her direction, because I felt 'She doesn't like me anymore'. But suddenly I heard her voice: 'Hey, what are you doing down there, Jimmy?' I looked up at her, and obviously she was in an agreeable mood, and I answered, 'I'm just sitting here in the sun, Marilyn.' Then she asked, 'Come with me, come on, Jimmy, I want to go right here into the liquor store.'

There was then a liquor store located on the immediate corner. 'I want to go in and buy some wine. I need some spending money, so I'm going to see if the man will let me write him a cheque for more than the amount of the wine, then I'll have the change . . .' Obviously she had spent her $40 spending allowance. So we went into the liquor store, and she was wearing that fur coat again, and she inquired about a certain bottled wine. The man behind the counter said, yes, he had it in stock, and Monroe requested 'three bottles, and may I write you a cheque for more than the amount of the purchase; would you give me the difference in cash, please?' He answered, 'Sure,' and I vividly recall Marilyn's hand sliding down into the pocket of her mink coat, she had such really beautiful hands, and I was just watching her hand now coming up out of the coat pocket with her chequebook in its grip. I was looking at her fingers, when suddenly the fingers let go of the chequebook and it dropped back down into the pocket of her mink coat. Marilyn then put her arm through mine, and with us now locked together, she whispered to me, 'We have to get out of here, Jimmy.' Monroe cancelled the wine order and arm-in-arm we departed the liquor store. Outside, I inquired at once, 'What happened in there, Marilyn?' She answered, 'I remembered that I was in the store last week, and when he asked me if I was Marilyn Monroe, I told him "No".' So in light of this, Norma Jeane had just realized that she couldn't exactly now produce Marilyn Monroe's chequebook.

JIMMY WAS THERE

While Monroe made her way around the city on her $40 a week, Haspiel then existed on a meagre salary of $28 a week. There was the day that we took a taxicab, and Marilyn wanted to go to an antique store called Lloyd's, between Lexington and Park Avenues, I think on East 61st Street. I was working as a messenger at that time, making very little money. In fact, I could barely afford to live on my wages. But it has been a lifelong component of my personality that I still want to be able to 'give back' in my relationships. I happened to have an available dollar bill on me this day, and remember that we are talking here about taxi fares of 1956. Anyway, Marilyn and I arrived at Lloyd's antique shop, and I readily seized the opportunity present and pushed my dollar bill into the cab driver's palm. Just as quickly, Marilyn demanded, 'No. No!', and I all but begged her, 'Please, Marilyn, please let me . . .', and she answered, 'No, absolutely not!', and she grabbed the dollar bill right out of the cab driver's hand. She then tried to give it back to me, and I refused it. Next thing I knew, Marilyn practically wrestled me to the floor of the cab, the two of us giggling wildly, and she shoved her hand down the front of my shirt. I remember her fingers coming to a halt just around my belly-button, where she let go of the now crumpled dollar bill, then pulled her hand back out of my shirt, put her laughter aside and shook a stern finger at me, admonishing her young Jimmy with the advice, 'You will never ride with me again, if you ever try to do that again, Jimmy!' She then paid the 75¢ taxi fare, and we proceeded into the antique shop. Needless to say, I never tried to pay her taxi fare again!

Now comes an incredibly mystical story that took place one morning up on 93rd Street. I was as certain to be there as was the Whelan's Drugstore on the corner. Now, when people do impressions of other people, they usually do their gestures, or what I call their 'ticks'. Marilyn had a tick: she would open the door at 155 East 93rd Street, and the first thing she did upon stepping out of it, *every time*, as she stepped out on to the street, she would cup her hand in front of her mouth and cough into it, then she would look up. You could count on this, you could bet the house on it. Well, there

Attending the Broadway opening of *Middle of the Night*. Kim Novak also attended the premiere that evening, turning around to stare at Marilyn throughout the intermission. Marilyn was capable of inspiring awe, even in other sex symbols.

came this morning when I wanted to see what would happen if I finally wasn't there for her. Although I was always there, whether or not I was always welcome, I never quite knew.

On the opposite corner of 93rd Street was a florist's shop, which had windows on both the avenue and on the side street, so that the set-up offered you the possibility of standing on Lexington Avenue and looking right through onto 93rd Street. I remember I was standing on the avenue, intentionally looking through the glass windows towards the side street, observing the doorway to number 155, when right on cue the door opened. Marilyn came out, she cupped her hand over her mouth and coughed. Then she looked up and took another step or so, and suddenly stopped dead in her tracks. She about-faced and headed back for the doorway, and I panicked, for no real reason – I just so loved seeing her! So I ran around the corner to catch up with her, but by the time I got into the block, she was already back inside the doorway, the door itself closed. As I headed towards the doorway, the door opened again, she emerged onto the sidewalk and – as I've already said, you could count on it – coughed into her hand and looked up, and then breathed a visible sigh of relief. Marilyn exclaimed, 'Oh, there you are, Jimmy!' This was a moment that bordered on the bizarre. She was so accustomed to coming out of the building to the sights of the fire hydrant that was there, the stop light on the corner, the drugstore; and, of course, 'Jimmy' was always there. Only this time Jimmy wasn't there! In some strange way, I think psychologically Marilyn didn't want to accept this, and when she had played the scene again, *Jimmy was there*; everything was in place and 'normal' again, if you will.

Jimmy was there, too, at Christmastime in 1955, when Marilyn asked if I would go with her to Sak's Fifth Avenue; she was going to do 'some shopping'. At that time, Six member Gloria Milone worked a block away from Sak's, in an office in nearby Rockefeller Centre. I already knew that Gloria had bought a Christmas gift for Marilyn, but I didn't know if she would have any real opportunity to deliver it in any personal way before December 25th. So, of course I'd said 'Yes' to Marilyn, and we had taken a taxicab down to Sak's Fifth Avenue. As we were about to enter Sak's, I advised, 'I want to make a telephone call, Marilyn, where will you be?', and she answered, 'I'll be at the men's tie counter, Jimmy.' I then departed in search of a payphone out on the street and called Milone, and asked, 'Gloria, do you have Marilyn's Christmas gift here in your office?' She answered, 'Yes, I do.' I said, 'Well, Marilyn is right down here, shopping at Sak's Fifth Avenue; perhaps you'd like to bring it down here and give it to her in person?' But Milone was unable to leave her office.

I then returned to Sak's doorway, and upon entering, what I saw was a mostly empty store, but at the men's tie counter were eight or nine salespeople, mostly males, all clustered before this small figure, who, I should tell you, was wearing a black teddy bear-style hip-length coat, black slacks nestled into black flat boots, her fabulous face ashine with nothing but hormone cream on its surface, and dark sunglasses hiding her luminous eyes. Obviously, Norma Jeane was trying her very best to not be 'Marilyn Monroe'. Yet every salesperson in the place was by now poised behind that tie counter, and nearly every other customer in the store, I would guess about sixty people, had clustered around the lone customer checking out the ties. She had been looking out for me, and as I came through the front door, Marilyn's face turned towards me, and she immediately made her way through the small sea of humanity engulfing her. She came right up to me, rising up on her toes to get as close as possible to my face, touched her fingers to her lovely lips and said in a distinct whisper, 'Shush. Don't say my name, Jimmy; I don't want anyone to know it's *me*.' Amazed, I thought to myself, 'Lady, you have lived for so long now in the middle of the crowd, you don't even see it anymore!' With everyone else present now staring at us, I thought, 'There's no one in this store who doesn't already know it's *you*!'

A day or so later it was a funny moment when the Six gave 'Mazzie' her Christmas gifts, and Marilyn apologized to one and all, 'I'm so sorry, I didn't get anything for you; I haven't worked all year.' We all laughed heartily at that line. 1955 was the year Monroe was 'on strike' from Twentieth Century-Fox Studios, the year she lived on an allowance of $40 a week.

That same Christmas and New Year's holiday week, Marilyn and I stood on the corner of 93rd Street and Lexington Avenue, and I had brought a piece of mistletoe with me. In the morning sunshine I asked her 'Close your eyes,' and she closed her eyes, and I literally nestled the mistletoe into Marilyn's hair. Then I said, 'Now open your eyes,' and when she opened her eyes, I told her, 'You're standing under the mistletoe, Marilyn!', and I took her in my arms and kissed her. A smiling Marilyn then reached up into her tousled blonde hair, removed the piece of mistletoe and pressed it into the palm of my hand, saying, 'Now, Jimmy, go and put it into your girlfriend's hair!' That very piece of mistletoe is still in my possession today. And, yes, I think I did manage to place mistletoe in Edith Pitts' hair for a holiday kiss, albeit another piece of the stuff.

It was at the onset of 1956, on January 3rd to be exact, that Marilyn made a strange request; 'Jimmy, be sure to pick up tomorrow's *Morning Telegraph* for me.' On perusal the following morning, I found in that newspaper an announcement that Monroe had finally settled her year-long differences with Twentieth Century-Fox. She had already signed a new contract with the studio on December 31st, and the event was publicly announced first in the *Morning Telegraph*, that Monroe was going to return to movie-making in Hollywood. I took a rare photo-image of her that same January, of the real Marilyn wearing her teddy bear-style coat, bell-bottomed trousers, and bobby-sox, walking down Lexington Avenue from 93rd Street. Soon she would be leaving the city and, boy, was I going to miss her!

February 8th, 1956, turned out to be quite a day. It started out with Marilyn inviting me to join her for coffee at the, by now memorable, marble counter in Whelan's Drugstore. We sat down on stools, and she ordered 'Coffee, please,' so I followed suit and ordered, 'Coffee, too,' and when the counterman walked away to get us our coffees, she called after him, 'No, no. Please give him milk; he's a growing boy!' It was to be a full quarter of a century before I would realize that that was a line from *Bus Stop*, the movie script Marilyn was studying at the time. It wasn't her line, it was another character's line, but it was from *Bus Stop*, nonetheless. And it took me twenty-five years and God knows how many viewings of the film before I finally noticed it. Method actors!

Moving on, from moving pictures to still images, there exists a rather sensational set of pictures, well-exploited shots of Monroe, taken by Milton Greene – black-and-whites of Marilyn wearing some lacy black underwear, along with a little bowler hat, and with a Charlie Chaplin kind of cane, shot against a stark black background. Well, these pictures must have been taken earlier that very week, because on that morning of the 'give him milk . . .', she had a manila envelope with her, and Marilyn asked me, 'Would you like to see some new pictures of me, Jimmy?' I answered, 'Sure!' She then said, 'Well, you have to look the other way while I prepare them.' So I looked the other way, and finally she said, 'Okay, you can look now, Jimmy.' I turned around to an unexpected vision of Marilyn sitting there with a contact sheet of perhaps ten photo-images before her, the item pinned to the counter by her elbow covering up one image, her thumb masking another, and even a paper napkin hiding yet another! It was all very 'gymnastic'-looking, and I was permitted to view the remaining frames, every one of them extremely racy for the era in which they were taken. Marilyn repeated these actions as she produced

Following her year-long self-imposed exile from Hollywood, Marilyn Monroe comes up victorious in these headlines announcing her brand new contract with Twentieth Century-Fox.

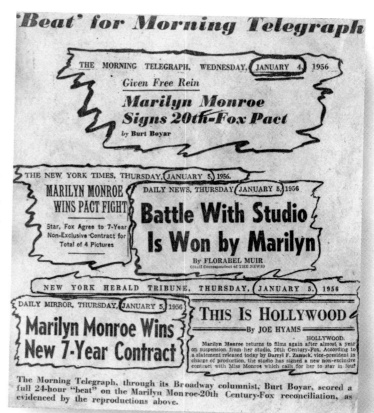

additional contact sheets for me to see. I was a young fellow on the brink of turning eighteen, and she was in her special way being a caring and responsible person, only allowing me to see certain frames, the 'tamer' ones.

That evening, Monroe attended the Broadway opening of *Middle of the Night*, at the Anta Theatre on West 52nd Street. I recall going into the theatre at intermission time that night. Marilyn was seated fifth row centre, and in the second row, way over to the side, sat actress Kim Novak who, during that entire intermission, was turned around in her seat and staring at Monroe. During the summer of 1955, Novak had written Monroe a nine-page letter, it was handwritten, asking her if there was any way that she could become involved in, be a part of Marilyn Monroe Productions. Years later, after Monroe had died, there was a very slick hardcover publication called *Eros*, and between its covers rested seventy-eight photographs of Monroe taken shortly before her demise, many of which Marilyn herself had put her 'X' on, meaning that she didn't want these particular images to be published. A friend of mine was with Kim Novak one evening when she was being shown a copy of *Eros*, and Kim became completely hysterical at the photographer's insensitivity, his obvious abuse of Marilyn by publishing the very photos Monroe didn't want seen. Despite Novak's tears, the photographs, taken by Bert Stern, were beautiful anyway; but Marilyn's wishes certainly should have been respected by Stern.

On February 9th, Monroe attended a press conference with Sir Laurence Olivier, where they announced that they would make a film together to be called *The Sleeping Prince*, later released as *The Prince and the Showgirl*. Following the press conference, Marilyn made her way up to East 93rd Street, keeping her afternoon appointment that day, after which I remember showing her some candid 8-mm film of her, in a little hand-crank viewer. Watching Marilyn with her eye pressed to the viewfinder, which was pointed skywards towards the light – it was still afternoon time – and her hand turning the crank-handle while moving images came back at her, those same images

Happy with the launch of her company, Marilyn Monroe Productions, she appears unperturbed when her strap breaks at the press conference on February 9th, 1956, to announce the forthcoming filming of the *The Prince and the Showgirl*.

dancing in my own head, I must have become really elated because Marilyn suddenly interrupted her viewing to say, 'Oh, Jimmy, don't get so *excited*!'

Later that same month, in February of 1956, I took what I feel is my most valued photograph of Marilyn, a colour shot of her standing on the corner of 93rd Street and Lexington Avenue. She is wearing her teddy bear coat over a skirt, white bobby sox and flat shoes, her polka-dot kerchief on her head, and she is holding a small black purse. It is a Marilyn I recognize instantly, as opposed to the public 'Marilyn'. This was an image I had longed to capture on film, so on that particularly chilly morning I hid myself in a nearby doorway and awaited the opportunity about to present itself. She appeared, she stepped into the street, I clicked the shutter on my Kodak Duaflex camera, she hailed a taxicab, and she was gone. And for me, a tiny bit of celluloid history was made; this image of her remains my personal favourite to this day. Over the many months of our meetings on 93rd Street, I had steadfastly abstained from bringing my camera to the area. But in the end, knowing that Marilyn would soon be off to Hollywood to film *Bus Stop*, and that this 'world' that we were currently sharing would be suddenly aborted, I couldn't resist the temptation to immortalize at least a moment of it for the future . . . and, can you blame me!

Just before my birthday on February 21st, the Monroe Six had gone to Marilyn and given her a store-bought birthday card in an envelope already addressed to J. R. Haspiel, 123 East 30th Street, New York, New York, a postage stamp affixed firmly to same, the only missing element being a single word needed inside the card, 'Marilyn'. And they approached her with the item and requested, 'All you have to do, Mazzie, is to sign the card and put it in a mailbox; it's for Jimmy's birthday next week.' I never received the card, and I didn't know about this incident until sometime later. Meanwhile, on my eighteenth birthday, the only thing that mattered to me in the whole world was to hear Marilyn say 'Happy Birthday' to me. So I put on the only suit I owned and departed my furnished room for 93rd Street, and there we were. I said to her, 'Marilyn, today is my eighteenth birthday, and I want you to be the first person to congratulate me.' And she stood there looking at me, and there was no response, none! I was thunderstruck. With a certain anger brewing inside me, I thought to myself, 'Is it so hard for you to simply look at somebody and say the words "Happy Birthday"?' I just couldn't believe what had happened; what had *not* happened.

Within a moment, Marilyn had hailed a taxicab and, having opened its passenger door, she stood there not unlike a chauffeur might. Looking over at me, after an eternity-like pause, she asked pointedly, 'Well, Jimmy, are you coming?' Marilyn was, after all, very much a magnet to me, so I got into the taxicab with her. Now, being the sort of person that I am, I was going to recover my dignity here. I had long harboured the desire to address her by her birth name, Norma Jeane, yet I had been hesitant ever to actually do that. But I thought to myself, 'Today is the day; my birthday present to myself is that I'm going to call her Norma Jeane!'

She was dropping me off at the corner of 58th Street and Lexington Avenue, my next stop being at 58th Street and Park Avenue, a block away, and she would then go on to her Sutton Place apartment. Well, the taxicab came to a halt at the curb of 58th Street, and the moment had arrived. I remember I looked into her face and said, 'So long,' and as I added the words 'Norma Jeane' I turned my face away from hers, unexpected emotions overtaking me, and I couldn't actually look at her! I had already opened the cab door for my escape, and as I was rising out of the cab, I heard a sort of whispered 'Jimmy' behind me, and my body, which was in motion leaving the cab, reversed the motion. As I sat back down into the seat, Marilyn put her arms around me and hugged me very tightly, and whispered into my ear, 'Happy Birthday, Jimmy', and then she kissed me. What had happened was that instead of being ordered to do something, like with the card from the Six, it had to actually come from her, or it wouldn't have been real for her. She could have said 'Happy Birthday' when I'd asked her to, and I would have been satisfied and never known the difference. But, to make it real for her, she had to allow for the vacuum of space in order to be herself and bring some originality to the moment. Needless to say, this was one eighteen-year-old who would never forget the day!

During that same month, the Marlon Brando–Frank Sinatra film version of *Guys and Dolls* was playing at the Capitol Theatre on Broadway. The producers had offered Monroe either of the two female leads in the film, parts now played on screen by Jean Simmons and Vivian Blaine, but Monroe's contract difficulties with Twentieth Century-Fox had prevented her from accepting the offer. Subsequently, on this February evening, the Six and I asked Marilyn if she wanted to go with us to see *Guys and Dolls*, and she answered, 'No,' asking, 'Why don't we go see *Umberto D*, instead?' For some reason now long forgotten, we didn't do it. Decades later, I finally saw the Italian classic, *Umberto D*, the title of which had remained with me all those years. Even though Marilyn was gone, I always knew that one day I would catch up with the film, even though we couldn't see it together. And so I sat there in a New York City revival house, the Thalia Theatre, sometime in the early 1980s, with the image of Marilyn still afloat in my brain as she had asked, 'Why don't we go see *Umberto D*, instead?' Well, in a way, we finally did, Marilyn. And, by the way, I loved it! Even more than *Guys and Dolls*.

On February 24th, the night before Marilyn left New York City, bound for Hollywood and the filming of *Bus Stop*, a member of the Six (I think, John Reilly) and myself went up to her apartment at 2 Sutton Place South, apartment 8E, taking with us seven 11 × 14-inch enlargement prints of the beautiful photograph that John Reilly had taken of Marilyn the night of January 7th, 1955, the shot of her in the elevator going to Marlene Dietrich's apartment. The goal of the visit was to get 'Mazzie' to inscribe these prints to each of the Monroe Six and to the 'Haspiel One', as I thought of myself, a sort of going-away memento from our adorable Marilyn. We were losing her, she was going away from us to make a movie, and we were all very insecure about this. We

This haunting picture of Marilyn captured on the night of January 7th, 1955, on her way to Marlene Dietrich's apartment, was inscribed especially for me by Marilyn just prior to leaving New York to film *Bus Stop*. It reads: 'To Jimmy, thanks for your friendship and devotion, Marilyn'.

As she leaves for Hollywood, Marilyn poses for me to take a picture amongst a sea of photographers (*clockwise*, Edith Pitts, Frieda Hull, John Reilly and Gloria Milone).

wanted her to inscribe something to each one of us on this extraordinary photograph!

I rang her doorbell, her maid opened the door, and Marilyn was at once visible, standing there just beyond the maid. She had on a figure-hugging, long-sleeved, high-necked black dress that she would wear on the plane to California the next morning, a dress that still had some pins in it, and she was trying on a very large black picture hat in her hallway mirror. We were welcomed in, and shortly thereafter we gave Marilyn the photographs, and she disappeared into her bedroom to write whatever she would write. Milton Greene was sitting in the living room, I would say in a somewhat inebriated condition, with one leg thrown over the side of his chair. There followed some polite conversation, then Marilyn emerged from her bedroom with the seven inscribed pictures. We wished her well on the movie, and took our leave of her sanctuary. Back downstairs, the photographs were handed out to their owners, each one of whom immediately checked to see what 'Mazzie' had written. On the photographs for the others, the Six, Marilyn had used the word 'loyal', or some form of it; on every one of them! 'Thank you for being so loyal', 'Thank you for your loyalty', 'Thank you for your loyalness', in all, a half-dozen variations of it. Mine was the only inscription that didn't contain that word and read: 'To Jimmy, Thanks for your friendship and devotion, Marilyn.' It felt very special to me that Marilyn had separated me from the Six in that unique way.

The next morning, when she travelled out to the airport, we followed behind her limousine in another car. I remember Marilyn rolling down her window as we sped along the Long Island Expressway, sticking her

As Reilly and Milone take more pictures, I wish Marilyn well on her trip in February 1956 to film *Bus Stop*.

head outside, and with her blonde hair billowing in the wind, she waved at us. At the airport, I became something of a human prop for the crowd of press photographers. While I was taking a shot of Marilyn, and she was posing especially for me, the press photographers shot the whole thing, and the following day a picture appeared in the centre spread of the New York *Sunday News* showing Marilyn and me together, along with Edith Pitts, Frieda Hull, John Reilly and Gloria Milone. The Collins kids were there, too, somewhere out of camera range.

Over the previous months, I had entered what was to become a twelve-year friendship with then Hollywood starlet and Broadway star Jayne Mansfield, and I was meeting Jayne later that afternoon at the theatre where she was playing 'Rita Marlowe' (That should read 'Marilyn Monroe'!) in *Will Success Spoil Rock Hunter?* While I was waiting for the time to pass that Saturday of Marilyn's departure, I found myself sitting on a stool in a luncheonette located directly across the street from the Belasco Theatre, having a cup of coffee at about five o'clock in the afternoon, when the NBC newscast came on the television in the luncheonette. And moments later, there we were; film of Marilyn and me walking hand-in-hand out to the ramp of the plane that morning! There were two other customers in the place, and the gent behind the counter, and the next thing they knew, I was standing up *on* the counter, yelling out 'That's me!' I was that taken aback by the moment, by the sight of the two of us on the television screen. Shortly, I enjoined with Jayne, who wanted to know all about the morning '. . . and Marilyn'. No pun intended, Mansfield was one of Monroe's bigger fans.

From Los Angeles, Monroe went on to Phoenix, Arizona for location work on *Bus Stop*. While she was still there in Phoenix, sometime in the middle of March, the Monroe Six and I were walking through the lobby of the Waldorf Astoria one evening, when they decided to telephone 'Mazzie'. So we proceeded to the bank of telephones in the lobby, and one of them placed the long distance call to Monroe. I was just there beside the caller as the telephone operator advised, 'Miss Monroe can't come to the

Before the plane departed,
Marilyn tossed these roses,
as mementos, to The
Monroe Six and The
Haspiel One.

phone right now; she's in the dining room with Josh Logan' (the film's director). Then I heard the caller say to the operator, 'Go and tell Miss Monroe that this is a person-to-person call from Jim Haspiel in New York City.' I was stunned. I felt that I had just been the set up for some spectacular kind of embarrassment when she *didn't* come to the phone! One usually tends to confront one's own insecurities, or lack of feelings of importance, or whatever, especially in such a potentially awkward situation as the one at hand, calling Marilyn on location.

An eternity followed, and then the operator came back on the line and said, 'Please tell Mr Haspiel that Miss Monroe said she'll be right here.' I couldn't believe it! And, that Marilyn came to the phone for me was actually secondary; I was still so mortified that they – I think it was Gloria Milone who had placed this call – had just done this to me, that I refused to take the phone, leaving a bewildered Marilyn at the other end of the line, now making polite chit-chat with the caller. In any event, on review, the fact that the caller opted to use the Haspiel name in order to get through to Marilyn certainly caused me to surface nicely in this potentially embarrassing moment. Perhaps the caller already knew something I was yet to learn.

Upon Monroe's June 2nd return to New York City, following the completion of *Bus Stop*, we all made our way out to the airport to meet her plane. I photographed a joyful and waving Marilyn greeting me from the ramp of the plane, Milton Greene and his friend David Maysles (the documentary film-maker) standing just behind her. She was to be back in our midst for only six weeks, but oh, how thrilling it would be!

Then there happened another of those moments when I didn't actually seek Marilyn out, when, unexpectedly, she simply appeared before my eyes. I was sitting on a stoop on West 23rd Street at eight-thirty one evening, when an unfamiliar light blue Cadillac convertible sailed by, driving in an eastward direction, with a blonde at the wheel – Marilyn! Never saw that car again, and what I didn't know at that time was that a certain writer lived up the block at the Chelsea Hotel, his name – Arthur Miller.

Elegant and sensual, Marilyn Monroe poses for reporters on her arrival in Hollywood to film *Bus Stop*. The woman I knew for eight years, was vastly different from this public persona.

Below: While dining with *Bus Stop* director, Josh Logan, Marilyn received a 'long distance call from Jim Haspiel', which was, in fact, from Six member, Gloria Milone, claiming to represent me. I was so stunned by this subterfuge I refused to take the phone from Gloria, leaving a bewildered Marilyn on the other end of the line!

Right: Director Logan emulating Marilyn's finger gesture to actor Don Murray, during this rehearsal for the final scene in *Bus Stop*.

Filming finally finished,
Marilyn returns to New
York. *Bus Stop* would be a
landmark in Marilyn's career
as a 'real actress'.

And the sightings continued. There was a night at the Belnord, the apartment building on West 86th Street, when the Six and I were sort of a staircase away from 'Mazzie' as she rang the door buzzer to the Strasberg apartment, and when the door opened, we overheard Marilyn greet someone with the Yiddish expression, 'Hi, bubela,' a term of endearment. And, no, we didn't hang out on staircases; we had followed 'Mazzie' there that night.

June 24th, 1956, turned out to be an incredible evening. The press was hounding Monroe and Arthur Miller, because by now the word was out that there was going to be a marriage. That night, Miller was trying to get Monroe out of the city and up to the quietude of the Connecticut countryside. Miller was driving a station wagon, now parked in front of 2 Sutton Place South; it was packed with Monroe's luggage, and the Press were keenly watching the station wagon like hawks. Suddenly, Miller came out of the building alone, got into the vehicle and quickly sped away. The reporters and photographers really weren't interested in him solo, they were interested in her, in *them*! So, the station wagon disappeared over to the area at York Avenue and 61st Street, to sit there in wait for Monroe. A taxicab was summoned to the parking alcove at 2 Sutton Place South, the passenger door now open and awaiting its next fare. Not unlike a blur, Marilyn suddenly appeared through the front door and bolted into the taxicab with flashbulbs lighting her way, and the cab took off.

The Monroe Six were not around that evening, and I was hanging out with Nathan Puckett, who had come to New York City from Michigan to see Marilyn, and was the president of one of Monroe's many fan clubs. Nate offered to pay for a taxicab to follow Marilyn's cab, so we took off after her, and one of the press photographers also followed. I vividly recall that Marilyn's taxicab pulled up to the west side of York Avenue at 61st Street; the station wagon was parked on the east side of the avenue, and the avenue was then (and probably still is) paved

Marilyn waves to me upon her return from Hollywood for a brief six weeks. Behind her stand photographer, Milton Greene (*left*), and documentary film-maker, David Maysles (*right*).

Marilyn attempts to disguise
herself in an effort to flee
reporters on the night of
June 24th, 1956, five days
before her marriage to
Arthur Miller.

with cobblestones. She got out of the cab, and she was running across the cobblestones in her very high heels, running through the oncoming traffic to reach the station wagon, with the lone press photographer in hot pursuit, and Nate and I sitting agog in our taxicab, some fifty feet away. Monroe raced around to the passenger side of the station wagon, Miller already gunning the motor, and as she reached for the door, the photographer got right up to her, put his hand on her shoulder and, with all of his muscle, swung Monroe around and threw her hard up against the side of the station wagon! She almost fell to the ground as he raised his camera to take a picture of her. Miller got out of the car and, paying no attention whatsoever to the press photographer, he simply assisted Marilyn into the station wagon, got himself back behind the wheel, and they took off, speeding up York Avenue. And we took off, too.

We drove through five red lights following the Miller vehicle, and finally at some point uptown, I think around 110th Street, the car entered onto the East River Drive, to go on to Connecticut. I had a subway token in my pocket, a 10¢ token, so I couldn't exactly go up to Connecticut! Our cab pulled over to the curb and (remember, it was still 1956) the meter read 95¢. Remember, too, that this driver had gone through five red lights for us, and now the young lad from Michigan, with no sign of city-savvy, handed him a single dollar bill, allowing, 'You can keep the change!' A nickel tip! As I recall, I hustled myself out of and away from that taxicab in a hurry.

Mentioning a press photographer cues up yet another unusual Monroe story, an event that I did not witness but one that was related to me by Peter Leonardi. Marilyn and Pete had gone down to Ratner's, a dairy restaurant on the lower east side of Manhattan, with some other people, and they had all had a drink or two, then something to eat, and Marilyn suddenly felt ill. Pete took her outside for some air, but a natural impulse overtook her, and Marilyn got herself over to the curbside and proceeded to vomit. She was leaning on the fender of a car, still bringing up vomit, when a flashbulb suddenly exploded in her direction; a press photographer following Monroe was now photographing this scene! At once, Leonardi went up to the photographer, wrested the camera from his hands and smashed it into pieces on the sidewalk. Had Pete not done this, we would have been subjected to a forever-picture-image of 'Marilyn Monroe vomiting'!

From drama to trauma: Marilyn invited me and the Six to 'come up to Roxbury, Connecticut on June 29th, I'll be giving a press conference there.' And so it was that the lot of us hitchhiked up to Connecticut for what was to become an extraordinary day in the life of Miss Monroe. In all, we had been in eight cars upon arriving at Arthur Miller's then house, located at Goldmine and Old Tophet Roads. There were cars all over the place, and reporters and photographers everywhere, but no sign of Marilyn. We were all milling about in the early morning warm sunshine when, suddenly, a station wagon pulled up and Marilyn jumped out of it, racing on her heels for the Miller house, her white blouse speckled with blood! Just behind Monroe and Miller, the driver of the vehicle, Arthur's brother Morton Miller, en route into the house, yelled out, 'There's been a terrible accident down the road!' At once, all of the reporters and press photographers started running down the road. I joined them, the Six stayed behind.

What we came upon was a car literally up a tree, its windshield smashed. In the centre of the road was a young man named Ira Slade, who was on his knees as we came on the scene, looking to the sky and praying to God. His kneecaps and his elbows, all four joints, were opened. He was the younger brother of Paul Slade, of *Paris Match* magazine, who was one of the professionals assigned to cover the event of the day, the Monroe-Miller press conference. He was accompanied by a female reporter, Mara Sherbatoff, who called herself a 'Princess', and who also worked for *Paris Match*; she was, I guess, to write the story and Paul Slade was to take the pictures. They had gone down the road towards Morton Miller's house, with Ira Slade at the wheel, in hopes of 'scooping' their fellow reporters and press photographers. Monroe and Miller were at Morton's house, and when they left there to go back and do the press conference at which they would announce their marriage plans, the Slade-Sherbatoff car took off after them. Of course, Miller was long familiar with the local back roads, with their hazard-spots, he drove them all the time. As the two autos rounded a curve, the car that Slade was driving close behind Miller's went right up into the tree, and Mara Sherbatoff flew into the car's windshield!

Miller realized that something had just happened behind him, so he stopped his vehicle and went back. Within moments Marilyn found herself helping pull the tragically injured Mara Sherbatoff off that shattered windshield. When I arrived at the sad scene, somebody was yelling, 'Get her a blanket; please, someone get some blankets!' By now, Mara was a pathetic figure on the ground, there beside the crashed car, its driver's side door ajar and opened over her still pulsating body. 'Get her a blanket, please . . .' Immediately, I turned around and ran on foot the mile or so back to the Miller house, and knocked loudly on the door, advising Arthur that 'We need a blanket!' He got me one; then, as I was heading on foot towards the roadway leading back to the site of the crash, Morton Miller called out to me, 'I'll drive you down.' We got into the same station wagon that Monroe had arrived in, and drove back to the scene.

Now, I had not yet looked at Sherbatoff close up, and all that I could see was that she was still there on the ground beside the car; in fact, this was not something that I wanted to see in any kind of detail. The reporters and press photographers had by now formed themselves into a horseshoe-like effect around the immediate scene, and they had obviously been recording the event, taking pictures of it now for more than twenty minutes. I took the blanket, and I remember starting at the beginning of this human horseshoe of professional people, asking each individual – while they were still shooting pictures – to take the blanket over. I couldn't elicit a response of any kind from any of them and, finally, having exhausted the entire group, I knew it had to be *me*. Damn it! And so it was that amidst the whirring sounds, the clicks of the cameras, I backed myself over to where Mara Sherbatoff lay dying.

The car door was still opened over her. I could see her feet and her legs, and using my own body, I pushed the door into a closed position. Then I rolled the blanket out and placed it over her feet, drawing it up along her legs. I was feeling very emotional, and very angry that all of these people who refused to respond to me just a minute ago were now photographing this moment, even filming it for the images I would see on television later that night. I had laid the blanket down over the lower portion of Mara's body when I noted her stomach, which was convulsing wildly, up and down. I had never before seen such a shocking sight! At that point, Paul Slade was holding Sherbatoff's head in his hands. Emotional and confused, I asked over my shoulder, 'Do you want me to cover her face?' He asked, 'What?', and I repeated, 'Do you want me to cover her face?'

It was all so terrible, with the cameras still whirring, my chest now filled with the kinds of feelings Marilyn must have felt a million times by now, in a million different ways! Raquel Welch once said 'Every time a flashbulb goes off in my direction, to me, it sounds just like a bullet!' I make the equation because, finally, I was feeling that horror of 'What are you guys doing over there? You know, this lady here is a human being; a person!' I remember making the mistake then of turning my head around, because Slade wasn't able to understand me, and while I was turning, I glanced downward at her and was suddenly stunned.

Photographer Paul Slade comforts his injured brother, Ira, as reporter, Mara Sherbatoff, lies dying after their car accident on June 29th, 1956, enroute to a press conference announcing Marilyn's forthcoming marriage to Arthur Miller.

From the centre of her upper lip to the top of her forehead, Mara was opened up from the impact of the crash, and the sounds of her almost quiet moaning, of her gurgling, were reaching up at me. As deftly as I could, I placed the blanket over her shoulders and feeling explosively ill, stumbled over to the side of the roadway and threw up, then fell down sobbing.

Back at Arthur's house, Miller had called for an ambulance and was told that there wouldn't be an ambulance on the scene for 'about two hours', at which point, Miller had fudged, 'I think you should know that that is Marilyn Monroe back there on the road, and this story will be on the front pages of every newspaper in the world tomorrow!' They got the message, and an ambulance was dispatched to the crash scene a whole lot faster! In any event, Mara Sherbatoff died several hours later on an operating table.

Anyway, a press conference of a different texture now ensued, from which there yet exists newsreel footage that is often used in Marilyn Monroe documentary-type films and television shows. There are moments of her talking that day, bits that are always shown just for 'what she is saying', without any explanation about the origin of the footage, with reporters asking her inane questions like, 'When are you going back to work, Miss Monroe?', and as she considers her answers, there are these obviously awkward pauses emanating from Marilyn, then, 'Yes, on July 13th I'm going to England . . .'. What today's viewers don't realize is that the pauses and the awkwardness are there in the footage because the person being asked these trivial questions has just had this truly horrible, life-altering experience, and with a plethora of emotions running rampant throughout her psyche, she is not really able to relate very efficiently to the bullshit being asked of her here. Woman to woman, she had to be thinking hard about the yet unknown fate of Mara Sherbatoff. So, the press conference did go on, and Monroe was being photographed, and being very much a professional, smiling for the ever-present movie and still cameras, when, in fact, *that* had just happened!

THE MONROE IMAGE

At this time, there was also that 'other blonde' in my life, Jayne Mansfield. It is a fact that I rehearsed Jayne's most important screen test with her, the test that ultimately won Mansfield her seven year contract with Twentieth Century-Fox. In a sense, during the latter part of 1955 and leading up to the fall of 1956, Jayne and I just about lived together; we spent nearly six nights a week from eleven o'clock until three, four, sometimes five in the morning together, always alone. This closeness allowed for a certain kind of intimacy. I remember vividly one personal dialogue when Jayne was so excited about the prospect of 'I'm going to Twentieth Century-Fox, Jimmy!' And I recall saying to her, 'You know, Jaynie, it's *not* going to work.' Surprised at my comment, she asked, 'Why, Jimmy?', and I advised, 'Because your face will not go to Cinemascope!' (a wide-screen process that was the current cinematic rage). From my own point of view, I was just being very realistic, telling Jayne, 'You don't really have Marilyn's beauty, even though you think you do, and, after all, we are in the era of the Ava Gardners and the Lana Turners, the beautiful faces!' Obviously, I was ultimately proven right, Jayne's face *didn't* 'go to Cinemascope'. That not withstanding, Fox did sign Mansfield.

I remember asking Marilyn one afternoon, 'How do you feel about Jayne Mansfield going to work at your studio, at Fox?' Now, I may sound like I'm always protecting Marilyn, but in reality, I promise you that I'm simply telling it all exactly as it originally happened; there was no trace of anger in Marilyn's soft-spoken response, she simply said in a low-key, matter-of-fact way, 'I just wish that she'd realize that there is room for everyone.' And Marilyn was saying this about a woman who was openly trying to walk away with her image, so to speak, trying at all times to *be* her. I found it very interesting that that was Marilyn's reaction to the certain prospect of Jayne Mansfield's coming presence on the sound stages at Fox. And I admired her for it, too. Besides, in the coming months, Marilyn had big fish to fry, indeed! While Jayne Mansfield would appear on local movie screens sharing her frames with Monroe's

Marilyn leaves for England to film *The Sleeping Prince* with Laurence Olivier. This film was later released as *The Prince and the Showgirl*.

139

former co-star of *The Seven Year Itch*, Tom Ewell, Marilyn would be sharing a sound-stage with the man she described as '. . . along with Marlon Brando, the greatest actor of our time!'

'Yes, on July 13th I'm going to England . . . and I'll be making *The Sleeping Prince* with Olivier.' That morning I met Marilyn up on 93rd Street, and other than the day of the press conference with Laurence Olivier, it was the only time that I ever saw her up in that neighbourhood with her make-up on – in this case, very nice, low-key make-up, and with light pink lipstick – and she was dressed very elegantly in casual clothing. We got into a taxicab, and with the rays of the morning sunshine playing on its windows, headed downtown. This was the era of taxicabs with no window-barriers between you and the driver; the driver really was right in there with you, and couldn't really help but overhear your conversation. But I somehow felt that it would be alright to talk to her in this 'public' atmosphere, to talk openly with her about 'Marilyn Monroe', whereas I would usually be utterly discreet about identifying Marilyn in any way to another person or persons who might be nearby us. Because she was about to portray a showgirl in *The Sleeping Prince*, it was on my mind, and I brought it up to her, the fact that she had played a showgirl in just about every movie that she had ever made. I then cited the fact that she played showgirls in *Love Happy*, *A Ticket to Tomahawk*, *We're Not Married*; she played actresses in *All About Eve* and *The Seven Year Itch*; that she had been a model in both *Right Cross* and *How to Marry a Millionaire*; that she had been a professional singer in the films *Ladies of the Chorus*, *Gentlemen Prefer Blondes*, *River of No Return*, *There's No Business Like Show Business*, and, most recently, in the just filmed *Bus Stop*. (And not only was *The Sleeping Prince* destined to be retitled *The Prince and the Showgirl*, but Monroe would round out her movie career by playing professional singers in *Some Like It Hot* and *Let's Make Love*, finishing up her showgirl-syndrome as a former, 'I used to dance in clubs', showgirl in *The Misfits*.)

We had gone through film after film, and finally the taxicab pulled into the parking

Producer and star, Marilyn
Monroe, plays opposite 'the
greatest actor of our time',
as the crew adds their
professional touches on the
set of *The Prince and the
Showgirl*.

alcove at 2 Sutton Place South. At once, a waiting press photographer approached the window on Marilyn's side, leaned down and said to her, 'Please don't run, Miss Monroe; I won't take any pictures.' Meanwhile, the meter read $1.05, and Marilyn was handing the driver two single dollar bills, when the driver looked at the two of us, me dressed in a simple shirt and jeans, and he asked a ridiculous question: 'Who's "Miss Monroe"?' In retrospect, it may be the dumbest question ever asked in the history of the world! She had her face – her 'Marilyn' face, that is – on, and we had just discussed the bulk of her motion picture career quite openly, the conversation itself liberally peppered with personal references.

There was a pause, then she answered, 'I am.' Then there was a longer pause, and he asked her, 'And *you* expect change?' After a shorter pause, she said, 'Yes, I do,' at which point he grudgingly gave her the 95¢ due. I felt like slapping her a moment later when she then gave him back two quarters for a tip. A quarter would have been more than generous at the time, and in this particular situation, *nothing* would have been much more appropriate! My displeasure tucked aside, I then gave Marilyn two kisses: one for her recent marriage to Arthur Miller (actually, two weddings took place; the first on June 29th, following the Mara Sherbatoff incident; the second at the beginning of July); the second kiss for 'Good luck on *The Sleeping Prince*, Marilyn!' Yes, I know; I should have said, 'Break a leg!', according to show-biz legend. In any event, the Millers departed for England that afternoon, the Monroe Six and the Haspiel One waving at the sky-bound plane.

Having completed filming on *The Prince and the Showgirl*, Monroe left England on November 20th, 1956, to return to the United States, to come back to New York City. I had hardly seen Marilyn for almost a year now, and the little Jimmy Haspiel inside me was by now convinced that he was 'the forgotten kid'. One night that December, I was with Jayne Mansfield, and we had her Great Dane dog, Lord Byron, with us. As Jayne was struggling with the animal, this person came running by us and yelled, 'Marilyn

Monroe is down the block at Sardi's restaurant!' Next thing I knew, I was headed straight down the block for Sardi's, Jayne somewhere back there behind me tugging at Lord Byron's leash. Awkward though the moment was, I was compelled to obey my primary instinct: I needed to take in the vision of Marilyn once more; it had been nearly five months since the last time I'd laid eyes on her! And, of course, no one would have understood my quick departure better than Jayne herself, a fact now well known to me.

The spreading word about Monroe's presence at Sardi's had caused a crowd to collect outside the restaurant. There was a huge fellow named Tony at the entrance to the place, who sort of doubled as a doorman-bouncer, protecting the celebrities coming and going from the establishment set in the heart of New York City's theatre district. Marilyn was just inside the front doorway, wearing her black suit with the fur collar, the collar pulled up to her cheek, and she looked wonderful. I had not seen her for so long, and now there were all these other people about, each one of them wanting to approach her, to touch her. And, very typical of me, I simply moved away from the crowd. There was a small theatre a door or so down from Sardi's called The Little Theatre, and I stood down there on the sidewalk curb by myself. Finally, Tony hailed a taxicab, opened the passenger door and summoned some guys to help him manage the crowd. He then got Monroe out of the door and through the screaming people – 'Marilyn, oh, my God! Marilyn!' – and into the safety zone of the taxicab, closing the door, waving goodnight to her. A small sea of humanity now charging the cab, the vehicle finally got free of the clawing crowd; and as it did, the window rolled down and her head came out of it, then her hand, and Marilyn waved and shouted, 'Goodnight, Jimmy!' And I didn't realize that she had seen me at all.

The next 'test of remembrance' came on the night of December 18th, at the movie premiere of *Baby Doll*, the Elia Kazan film starring Carroll Baker in the role originally offered to Monroe. Monroe had ordered a special gown for the opening, which did not arrive; so that afternoon of the premiere she went down to Eighth Avenue, and she purchased a gown right out of a display window. Pete Leonardi told me, 'She paid $87 for it.' By now, these decades later, everybody in the world has seen this particular gown because, in addition to wearing it to the *Baby Doll* premiere, Monroe subsequently wore the same garment to a well-publicized 'April In Paris' ball, and even more notably, in an advertising campaign for *The Prince and the Showgirl*, posing in the arms of Laurence Olivier. And I have to tell you that, although she looks sensational in it in pictures, she really didn't look that well in it in person. In fact, the garment made her look downright trampy, an unexpected vision of my angelic Marilyn that I had only this one time, fortunately. It didn't help her – what shall I call it – her projection here that as I gazed upon her stunning figure, her breasts were squeezing all too obviously out of the sides of the sequinned gown, challenging the insides of her upper arms for space, as it were. Simply put, the gown didn't fit her properly, and her bare bosom was pouring out of the sides of it! But in pictures, it looks great.

Later that night, I encountered Marilyn again at the Waldorf Astoria Hotel. Just outside the entrance to the Waldorf's Ballroom there was a bank of elevators, opposite which was a coat-check room, and I was standing about there, dressed in my only suit. There were a couple of hundred other people milling about the place, when an elevator door at the other end of this area opened, and a gorgeous Marilyn came swivelling out of it in this outrageous gown. Of course, there was the usual 'buzz' at her appearance, and the next thing I knew, I heard her calling across the crowd, 'Hi, Jimmy!' Now, do I have to tell you that about a hundred people suddenly looked around in my direction to see who the hell 'Jimmy' was? And with two hundred eyes now staring at me, at once I felt on the spot and conspicuous; but as I returned Marilyn's smiling greeting, to tell you the absolute truth, most of all, I felt a swell of pride ripple through my veins!

There was yet another social event held at the Waldorf Astoria Hotel, and while I no longer remember the reason for the evening, I cannot forget Marilyn's wonderful presence there that night. I was sitting in one of the ballroom's overhead boxes, the house lights were out, and Sammy Davis Jr was singing his heart out on the big, brightly lit stage. But I wasn't really looking at Davis, my own eyes trained keenly on a shadowy figure seated mid-way back in his audience, the person in that place who was being the most boisterous of all, shouting out titles of songs she wished to hear Davis sing; Monroe! Because the voice emanating from Marilyn was the girlish Norma Jeane's, the audience at large didn't really realize that it was Monroe who was being the spur. And if Norma Jeane was, as we have been told, innately shy, she was clearly absent from Marilyn Monroe's persona on this memorable night.

In January of 1957, the Arthur Millers moved into apartment 13E at 444 East 57th Street. An old telephone book of mine allows me to tell you that Marilyn's telephone number there was ELdorado 5–2325. In fact, Monroe was still the resident of 13E at the time of her death, having become by then a bi-coastal person. Anyway, there was an evening when I was with a friend over at the Harwyn Club, I think it was on East 52nd Street, and he was chatting with actress Kim Novak. As that socializing ended, I bid them goodnight, then walked by myself over to Sutton Place to see if Marilyn might be about. Once in the area, I struck up a conversation with a uniformed policeman, only to discover that he had taken Monroe to her building's entrance some minutes before my arrival: 'She came out about nine o'clock and asked me if I would mind sitting on a bench with her down there in the little park; I guess she was afraid people might bother her if she sat alone.' He added, 'She's a very nice lady.' I knew that, now he knew it, and of course, you know it! In telling this story, I do not mean to imply that Marilyn couldn't be alone; what I'm bringing up here is that as 'Marilyn Monroe', she couldn't really sit in the park alone, because there was no way to know what kind of a person might approach her there, no guarantee of safety, so to speak. So she had sat with the policeman in the small pocket park at the end of 57th Street, chatting while she watched the boats sailing along the East River, and he watched her, gathering for himself a memory for a lifetime.

There was another pocket park at the end of 58th Street, and Marilyn went over there one night, this time on her own, and she came upon two young boys who were capturing pigeons, trapping the birds in nets, then caging them. Marilyn asked the lads why they were doing this, and they informed her that they made money by catching pigeons and selling them to a meat market for 50¢ apiece. Marilyn then counted the pigeons thrashing desperately about the cage, and asked the boys, 'If I give you the money, will you free the birds?' They agreed, the cage was opened, and the pigeons took their leave. Marilyn then took the situation at hand a step further, arranging to meet these fellows on the nights they worked catching and caging pigeons at the end of which evenings she would pay them for the birds, then watch as they were released back into the air over the East River. Such was Marilyn's respect for the sanctity of life. And, no, this person did *not* take her own life; but that part of the story comes later!

There was one morning – I was still working as a messenger at the time – when it was raining out, and in that certain way that when you really love somebody, you always want to be protective towards them, I knew that Marilyn would be going up to 93rd Street in the downpour, and that I wasn't going to be up there that rainswept day. So, I managed to get a co-worker, Zelma, to lend me her umbrella 'for Marilyn', and just as I was arriving at 444 East 57th Street, Marilyn was en route out of the front door. We locked arms under the umbrella (why did I *know* that she wouldn't be carrying one?), and proceeded to hunt for a taxicab to take her uptown. A minute or so later, I spied an empty cab rolling towards us on the other side of the street, and said to her, 'Oh, Marilyn, there's one! Here, you take the umbrella,' and as I was running across the street in the rain, shouting 'Taxi!', I suddenly heard this delightful, incredible squeal just behind me, a sound like that squeal of victory one might make upon winning something against the odds there present. Marilyn could be not unlike a small child at times, and I turned immediately to see this little-girl face smiling richly at me and squealing because we had gotten her the taxicab!

Memories. Then there came a very magical moment. Let us remember here that the personage known to the entire world as 'Marilyn Monroe' was by now something of an enigma to me. From day one, the woman up there on the movie screen had nothing at all to do with the woman I'd met in person, absolutely *nothing*. Oddly enough, this was something I'd gotten used to very fast, mostly because the woman I now knew in person was so superior to the celluloid version who had so completely fascinated me from the silver screen. One day I was walking the real Marilyn, the flesh-and-blood version, home to 444 East 57th Street. On this particular day, Marilyn and I happened to be wearing matching black wool sweaters, unintentionally so, and she was just being Norma Jeane – there wasn't any essence of 'Marilyn Monroe' anywhere on her. Finally, we arrived at her building, and we paused outside and were in the midst of sharing what I would call a long 'so long' together. Somebody walking a dog happened by and stopped eight or nine feet away from us, and suddenly started staring at her; a neighbourhood person who had obviously now recognized Monroe. She was aware of him, and so was I. A minute or so passed by and someone else stopped, and a minute or so later there were three people, then four, then a couple walking by made it six.

All of a sudden Marilyn's head, which was usually in what I would call a normal position – well, her head started to tip backwards, and her smile, which was always an upwards smile, was now going in the other direction, and her laugh, which was always so very girlish, was somehow now dipping down into another tone. I was very taken aback by all of this, because I was literally watching her transformation into a person that I never ever saw when I was with her, a person that she never *put on* for me. I think that she really felt obliged to give the public 'Marilyn Monroe'. And she quite literally transformed herself into Monroe, without the high-gloss make-up, without the seductive evening gown, but everything else was in place; the persona, if you like. Her wide-eyed look distinctly absent, it was from now lidded eyes that Marilyn looked up at

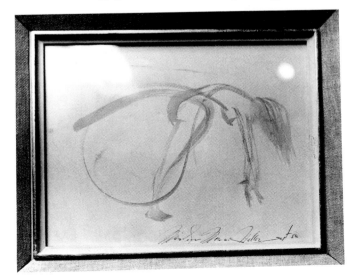

Monroe as artist is revealed in this 1956 sketch she called *Myself Exercising*.

147

me and in almost a whisper said, 'Jimmy, I think I have to go now . . .' Amazed, I looked into her face very pointedly and answered, 'I think you have to go too, Marilyn; I don't even know you!', because right then and there, I *didn't* anymore. To me, it was eminently clear what had happened here, that this 'character' that she had invented, and that was so successful for her, she simply *became*, in fact, at will. I think there is almost a sadness in the fact that she didn't trust the audience present, didn't trust that they would still love her as Norma Jeane. And they would have, because that is what they really loved about her, that underneath her marshmallow-image they could yet see that other person, and responded also to her. But 'Marilyn' never realized that.

Oh, yes; I still have the matching black wool sweater from that decades-ago day. Of course, it is by now but a tattered remnant, but one from a moment that remains ever fresh and vividly alive in my own memory. Norma Jeane into Marilyn; what a voyage to behold!

Still in 1957, Monroe and Miller bought a piece of property called 'the old Levenworth farm' on School House Road in Roxbury, Connecticut. It was two hundred acres, or three, depending on what reports you read (perhaps they added additional property later). Without saying it with any authority or specific knowledge, I think Marilyn actually bought the property that became their home away from New York City.

Hollywood, 1935: an unknown, lonely little girl sits on the edge of a simple cot in the dormitory of the local orphanage. Her name is Norma Jeane Mortenson. Connecticut, 1957: a world-renowned movie star peers out over the vast rolling hills of her property from the back porch of her newly acquired home. Her name is Marilyn Monroe Miller.

Times do change, and Marilyn was by now a person as different from the nine-year-old Norma Jeane as she was from the personage of her spectacular public image, as different as one could possibly imagine. Certainly an achiever, she was not weak, not negative, and most of all, not depressed. A depressed person wouldn't be out and about and going to acting classes every day; a depressed person usually goes and hides in a corner somewhere. In fact, she was nothing less than terrific! Yet the world doesn't really know this Marilyn, if only because they have been force-fed the other Marilyn for so long now. If, during her marriage to Arthur Miller, she was finally depressed, if that is the way he reflects on her, then maybe it was the result of something *he* was doing. I don't mean to imply that she was without blame in this situation, but this was one particularly strong and genuinely happy human being that I knew. Her exuberant personality said so too, and over the long term, you can't really fake that. Another way to look at it is this: what might she have been if she had had a strong foundation from the very beginning, how much more would she have been? Nonetheless, she was very strong, very much in command of herself, of her life. Norma Jeane was never accepted, she was cast out by everybody, but that was simply the circumstance. It was something that was happening in her life, but something that wasn't happening *because* of her, it happened *to* her. So following that, of course she wouldn't likely trust anybody to really care about Norma Jeane. On the other hand, she didn't have any trouble being the grown-up Norma Jeane with some people, but she still had to be 'Marilyn Monroe' for the strangers all about her – that was mandatory.

Meanwhile, back at the . . . Marilyn's homestead in Roxbury had its own little pond. I also recall that the living room had modern-style furnishings in it, none of the items what I would call particularly elegant or expensive-looking. And there was a 'nude' in the living room in the form of a small black statue, a female figure. Out back, just to the right of the main house, Monroe had had a separate studio built for Miller to do his writing in, kind of a small study. Life in the countryside didn't preclude trips to the city for Monroe, at least some of these excursions show-business oriented.

That May 12th, Marilyn went to Ebbet's Field in Brooklyn to kick out a soccer ball at some kind of charity benefit game being held there. A friend of mine named Tony

THE ULTIMATE LOOK AT THE LEGEND

Angelero lived a couple of blocks away from Monroe's apartment in New York City, and he was out walking his dog, passing by her building when he happened upon me. 'What are you doing here, Jim?' I told Tony, 'Well, Marilyn is going over to Ebbet's Field today, and we're [the Six and I] going there, too. Want to come along?' Actually, I already knew that Monroe had never particularly intrigued my friend Tony, but a minute or so later as she walked out of the building, her blonde hair worn shoulder length, her fabulous figure encased in a royal blue V-necked dress, her body language as alluring as ever, Tony got so excited at the sight of her that he grabbed his dog up into his arms and promptly jumped behind the wheel of the vehicle destined to deliver me and my friends to the stadium in Brooklyn! Now gunning the motor, Tony yelled to one and all, 'Come on!'

The stadium officials had supplied Monroe with a police escort to lead her car to Brooklyn, and as Tony watched the police car in front of Monroe's car swing over into the oncoming traffic lane, its sirens blaring, Angelero took the initiative and followed suit, moving in behind Monroe's vehicle. Thus we 'joined' her police escort for the trip to Ebbet's Field! And this was the guy, Tony, who less than an hour ago didn't think '. . . anything much of her; she's not so hot.' Arriving at the stadium, Marilyn now had to await her entrance cue; and so it was that we all gathered around her convertible for the next twenty minutes or so, Marilyn sitting there looking nothing less than ravishing, chatting and laughing, images of a budding legend that forever changed Tony Angelero's attitude towards my lady friend. Yes, I introduced Tony to Marilyn, and they shook hands, and like all human folk, Angelero threatened to 'never wash this palm again!'

In June, Marilyn invited me to Warner Brothers' screening room on West 43rd Street, to see her in *The Prince and the Showgirl*. Following the screening, she asked me, 'Jimmy, what did you think of my singing in the picture?' There was a song in the film, *I Found a Dream*, that she had sung in a voice quite different from the voice that had come off the screen in *Gentlemen Prefer Blondes*, in *There's No Business Like Show Business*; in fact, a voice she had never sung in before. Being the ever-truthful Jimmy Haspiel, I answered her, 'Well, Marilyn, I have to tell you that to me you sounded like Jane Powell singing at the bottom of a well!' She looked dismayed, but the bottom line here was that Marilyn could always count on me to give her an honest answer.

Marilyn's new singing voice was heard publicly for the first time when *The Prince and the Showgirl* premiered on June 13th, 1957, at New York City's Radio City Music Hall, the premiere itself a benefit for The Milk Fund. The post-premiere party that night was held in the Grand Ballroom of the Waldorf Astoria Hotel. At that party I looked on in amazement at Marilyn, who was dressed in a champagne-coloured evening gown that was so 'structured' that she came off looking not unlike a stunning version of Jayne Mansfield, such was the thrust of her bosom encased in the dress (Marilyn was a '36'; Jayne was a '40'), hovering quite rigidly above the tiniest waistline I'd ever seen on Monroe. Marilyn's figure was so exaggerated in the dress that the vision of her was nearly laughable. As she stood in front of you, you somehow knew that that dress on Marilyn could stand up all by itself! I was a bit mystified, because I knew for sure that with what she put into the dress, her natural hourglass figure, well, there was no need for her to wear a garment like that. And while Jayne Mansfield's career depended heavily on the Monroe-equation, this was the only time over the eight years of our friendship that Marilyn brought Jayne Mansfield to mind for me.

Un-cinched, Mrs Miller's waistline grew . . . and grew. On August 4th, 1957, I walked out of the Sherry-Netherland Hotel on Fifth Avenue, having just visited Jayne Mansfield there, and I headed over to 170 East End Avenue to visit Marilyn at Doctors Hospital. In the lobby, I pushed the elevator button, the door opened, and off stepped actress Lauren Bacall. I entered the cubicle and ascended

The other blonde in my life, Jayne Mansfield, finally won her seven-year contract with Twentieth Century-Fox. But although she was always trying to be another Monroe, Marilyn was generous in her comments about her imitator.

151

to Marilyn's floor, then made my way down the hospital corridor to her door. I tapped lightly on the slightly open door and awaited her voice. 'Come in.' When I entered her private room, the only illumination in there was the small light coming from the front of a radio on a nightstand just to the left of her. Classical music was playing on the radio, the sound itself low. Marilyn was lying in the bed, her lovely face minus make-up, the bedsheet pulled up to her chest. Arthur was sitting on a chair directly next to her; they were holding hands. Arthur stood up, he and I shook hands, and I visited with them for a few minutes, then took my leave. So this August 4th was to be one of the saddest days of her life, because she had just lost a baby boy, an already formed infant. This was the closest she ever came to achieving motherhood, and her great loss happened, uniquely, on the date that would mark her own demise.

The following day I sent Marilyn a get well card. Some weeks later, when I arrived home from my job – I was then living in a fifth-floor walk-up furnished room at 123 East 30th Street, and the superintendent used to leave the mail on a little table in the ground floor hallway – I walked into the hallway and there was this envelope in the pile of mail for 'Jim Haspiel'. I picked up the envelope and did what most people do, I searched its surface for a return address; there wasn't any. Suddenly, I noticed embossed letters on the surface of the beige-coloured envelope, and holding it in a certain way, the letters MARILYN MONROE loomed before me! At once, I ran five flights up the stairs to my room, because I knew I had to open this special envelope ever so meticulously, such was my reverence for the sender. It was with great excitement that I opened this missive from Marilyn and read the note contained within. Indeed, I was in a state of elevation to have received a letter from her and I read it once again. Perhaps I was too excited, for it wasn't until the third reading that I noticed the line that betrayed the sincerity of the special moment at hand.

As best I recollect, the now long-gone piece of paper read as follows, give or take a word: *Dear Jimmy — Thank you for the lovely card. It is so nice to know that there are so many*

Just days after Marilyn's miscarriage of her son in August 1957. This was the closest she ever came to achieving motherhood.

THE ULTIMATE LOOK AT THE LEGEND

people, whom I have never met, who think of me. Warm regards, Marilyn Monroe Miller.

It struck me suddenly that Monroe's secretary had actually written the letter. No 'happy birthday', so I'll call you 'Norma Jeane'! I decided to have some Haspiel-Monroe kind of fun result from this somewhat awkward situation. The very next time I visited with her, upon my departure I turned, looked her directly in the eye, and said, 'Oh, Marilyn, I want to thank you for the letter you sent me.' With an obviously puzzled look spreading across her face, Marilyn asked, 'What letter, Jimmy?' I answered, 'You know, Marilyn, that letter to all those people "whom I never met".' She quickly realized what had happened and just as quickly, Marilyn embraced me hard and pleaded, 'Oh, Jimmy, please forgive me; my secretary wrote that letter, she was responding to all those cards I received at the hospital.' Of course, there was nothing to forgive. And anyway, an embrace from the woman just now in my arms bested any letter from her, for sure.

Months passed. Then came the night of March 11th, 1958, a night to forget! This is a story that until this very moment was only told distortedly in the newspapers of the time, never before fully. That evening, one of Arthur Miller's plays, *The Crucible*, opened at an off-Broadway theatre in the Martinique Hotel on West 32nd Street and Broadway, in Manhattan. I was there with the Monroe Six that night. We were standing outside the hotel on the public sidewalk, and the Six were chatting away about something or other. A fellow came out of the hotel who turned out to be Miller's producer, Paul Libin, who then attempted to shoo the Six and me away from in front of the building, 'You're too loud, they can hear you in the theatre! Get out of here!' Just where were we supposed to go? For some reason, Libin took umbrage with me and came at me. When I attempted to walk away from him, he grabbed at the back of my brand new sweater, stretching the garment out of shape, and I swung around and punched him. Quickly, I got Libin into a grip in which I had his hands firmly trapped

Mr and Mrs Arthur Miller attend an Off-Broadway play, starring Arthur's sister, Joan Copeland, on November 18th, 1957.

THE ULTIMATE LOOK AT THE LEGEND

behind his back, both arms literally locked there. The only things I had left to work with were my teeth: I then proceeded to pick the back of his suit apart with my teeth. Having now destroyed his jacket and dress shirt, because I was so angry, as I let go of his arms, I quickly slipped my hands down into his pants pockets and pulled outwards, literally stripping Libin when his trousers fell down to his ankles! 'Fuck with me, will ya!!!' Having taken my sweet revenge, I then simply walked away, leaving a somewhat stunned Paul Libin standing there on the curbside.

Then it happened; on the next morning, I went out to get some breakfast, and passed a local newsstand. The image of Paul Libin was staring back at me from the front page of the *New York Post*! Yes, there he was again, bare to his waist and looking over his shoulder, displaying a small wound on his lower back for the press photographer. He also turned up in the other newspapers of that day, and all the stories claimed that on the previous evening he had been 'stabbed' by what he described as 'a hulking youth'. It was now my turn to be stunned! It was quickly obvious that Libin had lots of show-business savvy in him, having turned a possible nick from my teeth into a publicity bonanza for the opening of *The Crucible*. Marilyn never knew of my having to defend myself against her husband's producer that night.

I was just standing there,
waiting for a bus, when this
lady suddenly appeared out
of nowhere!!

MOVIES AND MEMENTOS

It was nearly three months later that I would take my first 'home movies' of Marilyn, 8-mm silent colour footage of her carrying a huge bouquet of flowers. It may have been the time of her next birthday, as she left 444 East 57th Street, heading towards a station wagon car with husband Arthur and the Morton Millers, all destined for the country, it seemed. In a close-up shot, you can read Marilyn's lips as she exclaims, 'I'm sleepy.' Over the next years I would shoot 8-mm footage of her on numerous occasions, thus not all of Marilyn Monroe's appearances on film were entirely professional.

Being in real-life close proximity to an individual from whom so many others wanted so very much, I too had an artefact on my mind, something I wanted from Marilyn; a pair of her sunglasses. Why? Possibly because they somehow symbolized the 'movie star' about her, the very thing that first brought 'Marilyn Monroe' to my attention. In any event, I had coveted this item for quite some time, more than once even asking her directly, 'Marilyn, I would love to have a pair of your old sunglasses sometime . . .' Finally, an afternoon came when, as I was standing and talking with the Monroe Six, Peter Leonardi, having just escorted Marilyn up to her apartment, came back downstairs holding up a pair of her sunglasses, and asking, 'Who gets these?' They were obviously meant for me, but an aggressive Gloria Milone rushed past me and grabbed them right out of Peter's hands! Thus, I never did get the sunglasses. And right then and there, I wanted to erase Milone on the spot! So, Glo, not unlike the hundred and thirty-seven trees now living on my property out on the Island, trees that I'm 'minding' for a higher power, I just want you to realize that even today I consider it obvious, given Marilyn's original intent, that you're 'minding' the sunglasses for me!

On July 8th, 1958, Marilyn made her way to the airport to return to Hollywood for the filming of *Some Like It Hot*, and I took colour shots of her and Arthur there. About *Some Like It Hot*, it might be noted that her greatest film success, publicly speaking, began filming on a date that, if one traces Monroe's history, looms up frequently as a day for her to reckon with, that date being August 4th. Anyway, subsequently,

On arrival in Hollywood, a dazzling Marilyn sits in her hotel room, looking forward to filming *Some Like It Hot* with Tony Curtis and Jack Lemmon.

Marilyn invited me to a sneak preview of the film held at the Loew's Lexington Theatre on February 5th, 1959, a screening also attended by Marilyn and Arthur Miller, now back in New York City.

It was three years since I had asked Marilyn to congratulate me upon turning eighteen years old, and those thirty-six months had obviously escalated the rapport between us, as evidenced by her invitation to me on February 25th (four days after my twenty-first birthday) to 'Come by tomorrow evening, Jimmy, and we can take a picture of me giving you a birthday kiss!' Now, I don't know anybody out there who would have refused this offer, so I put on my best slacks, a dress shirt and tie, and a sports jacket, and returned to Marilyn's abode on the 26th all smiles. As it turned out, that was the night that Monroe belatedly picked up her Crystal Star Award, the French equivalent of the Academy Award, as Best Foreign Actress for *The Prince and the Showgirl*. Subsequent to the awards ceremony, when she arrived home, I remember that it was the first time (and the only time) that I ever saw Marilyn act like a movie star away from the crowd. Emerging from the car, Marilyn actually dragged her mink coat along the street and up the curb. As Arthur led her into the building, she advised him, 'It's Jimmy's birthday and I have to give him a kiss, Arthur.' Soon enough, my arm was around Marilyn's waist, our bodies pressed tightly together, and as Miller attempted to mask the scowl-like expression coming onto his face, three people began shooting flash pictures. An autograph collector named Walter Horoshko had joined Frieda Hull and Eileen Collins behind the camera lens to record the moment as Marilyn proceeded to plant a birthday kiss on me. And, having done so, Marilyn then examined my cheek, exclaiming, 'Oh, I didn't leave a lip print, Jimmy,' then kissed me a second time, being sure to leave the outline of her lips firmly affixed to my skin. As I let go of her waist, Marilyn came back at me yet another time, put her arms around me, squeezed me hard, and whispered into my ear in a most endearing way, 'I remember when you were seventeen, Jimmy!'

If you had telephoned
Hollywood 7-5111,
extension 439, on August
7th, 1958 . . .

Costume tests and rehearsals
are under way for *Some Like
It Hot* with Marilyn in the
character of Sugar. The tall
hat (*left*) never made it into
the final film.

Resting on the location set of *Some Like It Hot*, with Arthur Miller, and acting coach and friend, Paula Strasberg.

Opposite: An umbrella protecting her from the sun ('I like to feel blonde all over'), Marilyn chats with her husband between takes.

A playful Marilyn made sure that she left a lipstick imprint of her lips when she gave me my twenty-first birthday kiss.

Soon came the sensational night of the premiere of *Some Like It Hot*, March 28th. I took wonderful colour slides of Marilyn as she left her apartment to go to the newly renovated Loew's State Theatre on Broadway that evening. I also photographed her some two-and-a-half hours later at the post-premiere party held at Lee and Paula Strasberg's apartment at 135 Central Park West.

An interesting sidebar to this event is that in the book by Lena Pepitone, Monroe's 'maid', *Marilyn Monroe Confidential*, Pepitone reports watching a horrified Monroe reacting to the premiere screening of *Some Like It Hot* that night, a Monroe who rushes from the Loew's State Theatre back to her apartment, where Lena finds her undressed, screaming 'Disgusting! Disgusting!' about her new film. Let us remember here that Marilyn had already seen the film at least once that I know of for sure, at the preview screening on February 5th, therefore its content could hardly have surprised Marilyn on the night of March 28th! Pepitone's overblown tale becomes even more suspect from the fact that minutes after the screening's conclusion, Marilyn was immediately over on Central Park West putting her quite sublime imprint on the celluloid in my camera! So, the question arises: who the hell was Lena gawking at? Arthur Miller escorted Marilyn both to the premiere and to the party afterwards, and they stayed long into the night at the Strasberg bash. Perhaps the 'maid' fell asleep and dreamt her version while awaiting the return of her employer. Of course, any reasonable person might pose the question, who to believe, Pepitone or Haspiel? Well, the obvious answer in this particular instance lies in the indisputable, the still lovely colour images captured by my own amateur lens on the night of March 28th, 1959.

At that time there were extended-play record albums called 'EPs', small discs usually containing four songs from a motion picture soundtrack. So, in addition to the full soundtrack album released from *Some Like It Hot*, United Artists Records decided to release a separate disc, an EP version featuring just those songs from the film that were sung on screen by Marilyn Monroe. There were three numbers in all, *Running Wild*, *I Wanna Be Loved By You*, and *I'm Thru with Love*. To round out the EP, Monroe recorded a fourth song, a title number, *Some Like It Hot*. We eagerly awaited the release of this EP featuring Monroe's new song. Finally the record came out, and Marilyn asked me, 'Would you please pick me up a copy, Jimmy?' Of course, I did, and the cost of this disc was $1.63, which I mention for a specific reason. Approaching her apartment building, the record and

The Millers join in the laughter as they watch the public preview of *Some Like It Hot* on February 5th, 1959. *Right:* Leaving home for the film's premiere on the night of March 28th.

receipt in my hand, I happened upon Marilyn's stepchildren, Jane and Bobby Miller, and I gave them the items: 'Give this to your stepmother, please.' When I saw her subsequent to that, I asked Marilyn, 'Did you get your album?' I remember that we were in the middle of an embrace when I asked her this, we were being physically close, and she answered, 'Yes, I did, Jimmy,' and she was now squeezing me and thanking me. The pauper that I was at the time was also in her embrace, and I still remember vividly how my hand rose up between our blending bodies, rising up to just under her chin, my palm extended towards Marilyn as I requested, '$1.63, please!' She then produced her change purse and counted out the amount due me to the very last penny, depositing an exact $1.63 into my hand coin by coin. It might also be noted here that, unlike her previous query regarding my opinion of her rendering of *I Found a Dream*, Marilyn exhibited no such interest as to my thoughts about her warbling of *Some Like It Hot*. It was just as well, given that the recording didn't really impress me.

That May 13th, Monroe received the David di Donatello Award, Italy's 'Oscar', again belatedly for *The Prince and the Show-girl*, as Best Foreign Actress. The presentation was made at the Italian Consulate at 686 Park Avenue, at 68th Street. I took 8-mm colour film of Marilyn as she arrived for the ceremonies, then continued filming her inside the Consulate as actress Anna Magnani awkwardly jostled an umbrella in one hand and a paper bag in the other, then surrendered these items to a nearby individual in order to bestow on Monroe her award. All of these images passed onto a piece of celluloid that charms viewers to this very day.

Opposite: Marilyn's arrival at the Italian Consulate in New York, for the bestowal of the David di Donatello Award (Italy's 'Oscar'), which was given to Marilyn for her performance in *The Prince and the Showgirl*.

An especially alluring Marilyn poses for me on the night of the *Some Like It Hot* premiere.

Arthur Miller is seen
following Marilyn from the
Actors Studio in 1959.

Following the ceremony, Marilyn
departed the Italian Consulate and went
directly to an acting class being held in the
Capitol Theatre Building over on Broadway and 51st Street, where my 8-mm
movie camera gathered even more Monroe footage for the Haspiel archives. By this
time a light rain had begun to fall, and the film footage shows Marilyn being escorted
back to her limousine under the protection of her chauffeur's umbrella, following the
class. I took still photos of Marilyn later that same month over at the Actors Studio, this
time out with Arthur Miller and actor Montgomery Clift, soon to share the movie
screen with Monroe in Miller's *The Misfits*.

Then came the afternoon of June 1st, 1959, Marilyn's thirty-third birthday. I took
some wonderful home movies of her that afternoon as she left 444 East 57th Street to
run an errand, then again when she returned home. Memory assures me that Marilyn
was wearing an orange summer dress, white heels, a thin kerchief on her head, and a
beige raincoat over her shoulders. Memory, I say, because this time out my home
movie camera was loaded with black and white film. In these movies, on her return
home, Marilyn is carrying a very large cake box, obviously containing her own birthday cake. Decades passed before it finally struck me on watching the footage that
Marilyn (Norma Jeane!) had had to go and pick up her own birthday cake! If it's your
'day', your party, then perhaps someone else ought to fetch the cake; where was Arthur
for this errand? Better yet, where was 'maid' Lena? In any event, Marilyn was a doll
that day, even 'projecting' a big close-up kiss into the lens of my trusty home movie
camera. If 'a picture is worth a thousand words', how priceless these images must be!

Not all of my celluloid keepsakes evoke memories as regards the taking of them,
the circumstances surrounding the images. Three days after her birthday, on June 4th, I
photographed Marilyn again, this time by way of a colour slide that depicts her wearing

Opposite: Marilyn
affectionately greets her
friend, Shelley Winters, at a
party in 1960. Before the
decade's end, Shelley would
play the role of 'godmother'
to my sons, Dean and
Michael.

a black top and white pedal-pushers, a moment about which no memory survives but the slide itself, dated on the border of its frame. Then there is some 8-mm colour film that I took of her wearing a white kerchief and a checkered coat, in which Marilyn is smiling at me and gently waving at the lens with her right hand. That July 9th, I took more colour film of her as she was exiting a taxicab at 444 East 57th Street, film in which, if you slow-motion the images, it's incredible to watch the way Marilyn almost dances ever so sensuously past the camera's lens, smiling lovingly into it at the same time.

Not all of the photographs of Marilyn currently resting about my home had been taken by me personally. A friend of mine named Phil Claude had given me a shot of Marilyn taken the night she filmed her famous 'skirt-blowing' scene for the screen version of *The Seven Year Itch*, this particular picture having won a prize of some kind in a photo competition. I took the valued image to Marilyn on the night of my twenty-second birthday, and she inscribed it as follows:

> *For the one and <u>only</u>,*
> *<u>Jimmy</u>, my friend,*
> *Love you,*
> *Marilyn*

Her underlining the words 'only' and 'Jimmy' lent a special poignancy to the inscription.

More images-without-memories: there exists some 8-mm colour film that I took of Marilyn holding some strange dog (not her beloved Hugo) on a leash. During this same period, I shot film of Marilyn dressed in a very sexy V-necked blue dress covered in white polka dots, her beige raincoat again draped casually over her shoulders, as she embarked on an evening out with Frank Taylor, the coming producer of *The Misfits*.

Marilyn invited me and the Six to come to the Twentieth Century-Fox soundstage

Marilyn inscribed this famous picture taken during the 'skirt sequence' for *The Seven Year Itch*.

in New York City to watch her 'film some costume tests for *The Misfits*, Jimmy.' We arrived at the studio, and once inside, we could see her standing there on the soundstage being filmed in the bluejeans and sleeveless white blouse she would later wear in the movie. For some by now long forgotten reason, I was uncomfortable in there and I opted to go back outside. Subsequently, when Marilyn emerged from the Fox-Movietone building, I began shooting some 8-mm colour film of her as she gestured towards me, smiling, glancing over her shoulder as she now undulated across the street to a waiting car. Moments later sitting inside it with husband Arthur, members of the Six requested that she 'Come back out again, Mazzie, so we can all take some pictures of you.' Marilyn begged off with the line, 'No, I can't, I'm not feeling well,' and one more time my notable temper reared its ugly head; I went over to the open car window and reminded her, 'For Christ's sake, Marilyn, you asked us down here, you know, I wouldn't have come . . .' I was still in mid-sentence when Marilyn looked over at Miller, telling him, 'I have to get out of the car, Arthur; Jimmy wants to take my picture.'

Thus, where the pleas of the Six had failed, she now opened the door and stepped out of the car, asking, 'Where do you want me, Jimmy?' Searching the immediate area for a prime spot, I answered, 'Right up there on that stoop, Marilyn.' The stoop, a cruddy affair in an obvious state of disrepair, now supported a marvellous Marilyn primping before my lens, outfitted from head to toe in beige, her blouse and skirt and high heels all extending the lustrous look of her wonderful hair ('I like to feel blonde all over!'). 'I'm shooting you in a full close-up, Marilyn . . . Profile, please, Marilyn . . . now the other side, Marilyn . . . Now, let's do a full-length pan shot, Marilyn.' And, finally, 'Let me come up there, Marilyn, so Frieda can shoot us together.' We then chatted away as Frieda Hull manned my home movie camera, then Marilyn stepped down off the stoop at 453 West 54th Street to return to the car and Miller. Subsequently, when I ran this footage for writer Maurice Zolotow in 1961, the Monroe biographer was very much impressed by the sight of *The Misfits'* black-and-white Marilyn now in glorious colour, opining, 'She's just incredibly beautiful! They should've shot the movie in colour; *you* should've been the cameraman on *The Misfits*, Jim!'

Following her costume tests for *The Misfits*, Marilyn returned to her apartment, where the Six and I shortly caught up with her. I was shooting additional 8-mm colour movies of a very different Marilyn probably within an hour of the West 54th Street footage. This time Marilyn was about to run an errand, her earlier hairstyle completely gone, her hair now pulled back under a beige kerchief, the beige heels now replaced by flat shoes, a summer coat draped over the beige blouse and skirt; finally, a Marilyn bearing little resemblance to the lady of *The Misfits*. Her 'Marilyn Monroe' mask was officially off, and Norma Jeane was now off to a local store to fetch something, a red thermos bottle in her hand. The date was July 8th, 1960.

On July 17th, Monroe went to the airport to fly out to make *The Misfits*. It was to be the second time, the last time, in all those years that I saw her that she was looking bad. So bad, in fact, that as I went up to her as she was about to board the plane, she turned to me, and I took one look at her ravaged face and refused to accept what my eyes could see so clearly. I turned away from her. I literally turned away from her! Also, as she was running to board the plane, there were several menstrual stains visible on the lower half of the back of her beige skirt (at this juncture, I was shooting 8-mm colour film of her race for the plane). I knew that she had extremely painful periods, so she had obviously had a very bad night. In fact, as I looked into her face for a moment at the entrance to the plane, what so disturbed me were the bags under her eyes – bags that are under my eyes right now, but I'm fifty-three years old! She looked awful and, emotionally speaking, I just needed to reject this image of her on the spot.

Above: An embrace for Clark Gable as the filming of *The Misfits* winds up. Ten days later, Gable was dead from a heart attack.

Opposite: Marilyn invited me and the Monroe Six to costume tests for the *The Misfits* on July 8th, 1960, after which we took our own pictures (*right*).

THE SHOWGIRL AND THE PRESIDENT

Monroe divorced Miller on January 20th, 1961. Eleven nights later, she attended a sneak preview screening of their film, *The Misfits*, held at the Capitol Theatre on Broadway. The film opened at the Capitol on February 1st, and I went to see it with eager anticipation, with only the highest hopes for Marilyn's success. But what happened as the film unfolded up there on the big screen was that a quiet anger was building up inside me, an anger focused on Marilyn from the onset of the film. What the hell did I care about Clark Gable, about Montgomery Clift; and to be real about it, I didn't give a damn about Arthur Miller, either. I had expected so very much from *The Misfits*, from her! But now I was being devastated by what I was seeing. At the point in the film when Monroe played her most dramatic scene – and it had been photographed with her shouting, screaming her lines a great distance away from the camera's lens – well, this one scene made me so angry that when the film concluded and I departed the Capitol Theatre, I headed straight for the pay telephone on the corner of 51st Street and Broadway, popped a coin into the slot, and dialed EL 5–2325, intent on telling my 'method actress' friend off! Extremely presumptuous of me, to be sure, but that's exactly what I did. It so happened that Marilyn wasn't home. Of course, in retrospect, I'm more than glad the phone rang on unanswered. And, in later years I would come to understand the brilliant calibre of Marilyn's performance in *The Misfits*, ultimately championing her splendid work in this motion picture.

The day after I saw the film, its newly divorced star entered the Payne Whitney Psychiatric Clinic on East 68th Street, and shortly went from there over to the Columbia Presbyterian Medical Centre on New York City's upper west side, seeking help as regarding her by now obvious problems with prescription drugs. Monroe went there in an effort to withdraw from her usage of sleeping pills, which she had begun taking around 1947–8. Obviously it starts with one, but by 1960 she was taking, so I was told, sometimes twenty sleeping pills a night! Certainly this dosage, even a lot less, would kill me; would kill nearly any one of you. So, finally, the situation had become critical.

Attending the preview of
The Misfits in New York in
1961. Shortly afterwards,
Marilyn entered the
Columbia Presbyterian
Medical Center to overcome
her problem with sleeping
pills.

Monroe's associates were by now waking her up in the mornings by pouring hot coffee into her until she rallied. So she went into the hospital to withdraw from these pills, and remained there for the next twenty-three days.

I didn't see Marilyn again until March 5th, when she departed Columbia Presbyterian Medical Centre in what turned into an all-out riot of media people, and more than a hundred everyday citizens who showed up for the event. From this occasion there exists sound newsreel film of reporters screaming at policemen to get out of their way, in the reporters' quest to get at Monroe, when all the cops are really doing is attempting to protect Monroe from the out-of-control mass of humanity now lunging at her. 'Officer, get out of the way!', 'Officer, duck down!' And while these black-and-white newsreels are still amazing to watch and listen to, so too is my own home movie camera footage from that day, the entire obscenity captured on 8-mm in glorious colour – priceless film imagery.

Author Maurice Zolotow had recently written the first full-length, real biography of the world's most famous blonde (*Marilyn Monroe*). There were books and cover-to-cover magazines about her during her lifetime, but Zolotow's was the first full-blown hardcover biography of Monroe. I had read the galley proofs of the book, and I had written to the author, sending him pages of typewritten notes to state, in effect, that 'you are wrong about this'. I had been sure to limit myself to those items about which I could bring proof to my versions. My letter did not actually solicit any response from Mr Zolotow. Because I knew that Marilyn was very unhappy about the book, I simply ended my comments to Zolotow with a rhetorical question: 'Is it possible that you have done Miss Monroe an injustice here?'

Zolotow sent me a letter back, defending his work, advising, 'Billy Wilder told me this . . .' and 'Walter Winchell told me that . . .', and so on. As I read Zolotow's letter, I thought to myself, 'So what, a fact is but a fact. It doesn't really matter what anybody else tells you, as her biographer, you set yourself the responsibility to tell her story with

Marilyn and ex-husband, Joe DiMaggio, seen leaving a Florida motel in March 1961, which started rumours of a re-marriage. Joe never got over Marilyn and they remained close friends until her death.

truth.' Anyway, Zolotow ended his missive with the line, 'but every writer loves to have readers like yourself, and I would like to take you to lunch sometime. Would you please give me a call?' I thought, alright, I'll call him; it's not that I want to go to lunch, 'but I do want to show you what I'm talking about'.

Zolotow invited me to join him for a repast at Sardi's Restaurant. I declined, allowing, 'I don't think that I could really discuss this subject with you in a public place, surrounded by other people. Why don't you come over to my place, instead?' Understanding my point, his interest still intact, he asked, 'When?' I answered, 'Well, the Academy Awards are on television this coming Monday evening; would you care to come here earlier so that we can talk about Monroe, then, if you'd care to, you can stay and watch the awards telecast here?' Zolotow accepted the invitation. It was Thursday night, and I had lots to prepare before Monday arrived.

I spent hours over that weekend at what I affectionately thought of as 'the Marilyn Monroe Museum', Frieda Hull's house, and it was from there that I culled a good deal of the 'evidence' that I wanted to present to Zolotow. On the afternoon of the evening on which he was to visit, I made my way over to the British Book Centre in New York City, and I purchased the British edition of Zolotow's book, an edition which was extended by an additional chapter about the period surrounding *The Misfits*. It was an impressive-looking version of the book with gold embossing on it, and I decided I'd probably want the author to inscribe it to me later that day. I thought to myself, 'Well, when Zolotow arrives, if you hand the book to him then, he's going to write something not far removed from what he might write to a stranger on the street. Wouldn't it be better to risk waiting until the evening's end, when he might write you something with meaning behind it, instead, something with substance; or, he might not write anything at all?'

Zolotow came in, we socialized for a time, and then I began the process of presenting to Maurice the absolute proof of every fact that I had challenged him on in my letter suggesting his 'injustice' to his subject, Miss Monroe. Point by point, I erased from Zolotow's mind his versions of any number of 'facts' about my lady friend that I could prove were false.

Hours passed and, in fact, we never did watch the telecast of the Academy Awards. Finally, at the end of the long evening, Maurice said to me, 'Jim, you would probably be interested in the British edition of my book; it just came out this week, and it contains an extra chapter, as well as Marilyn's calendar pictures' (not permitted in the American edition), at which point, I reached behind my chair to an end table shelf, and I responded, 'Actually, I went out and bought a copy this afternoon, Maurice.' Holding the volume in my hand, I then asked, 'Would you consider writing something in this to me?' Without a pause, Maurice answered, 'I certainly would.' Maurice then took the book and wrote in it. I ask the reader's patience here . . .

On June 14th, Marilyn returned from Hollywood, and she was with Ralph Roberts, her masseur and good friend. We greeted. I had the Zolotow book with me. I knew well by this time that the book was a sore subject with her, that it wasn't something you could bring up lightly, surely not an item you would place before her face. Regardless, I chose to tell her in detail the story of Maurice Zolotow's visit to my home, about my letter to him and all that had followed because of the tone of it. By the time I had finished telling her the story, Marilyn's nose was quite literally inches from mine, her beautiful eyes very wide open, and she asked, 'What did he write in the book, Jimmy?' That was the signal I was waiting for, so I produced the volume, suggesting, 'Why don't you read what he wrote to me, Marilyn?' She took the book from my hand and read Zolotow's inscription, a look of satisfaction, of victory coming upon her face. It was then that I dared ask, 'Would you sign it, too, Marilyn?' She turned to Roberts, asking, 'Do you have a pen, Ralph?' He reached into his jacket pocket and passed a pen to her, then Marilyn looked me square in the eyes and advised, 'This is the *only one* I'll ever write in, Jimmy!', the pen pointed at me for obvious emphasis, her words edged with genuine determination, and she wrote. The page reads as follows:

> *To Jim Haspiel —*
> *who could have*
> *written a better*
> *book on MM —*
> *sincerely*
> *Maurice*
> *Zolotow*

– to which the flesh and blood personage outside of the book added:

> *Thats right!*
> *Marilyn Monroe*
>   *x o x o [kisses and hugs to me]*

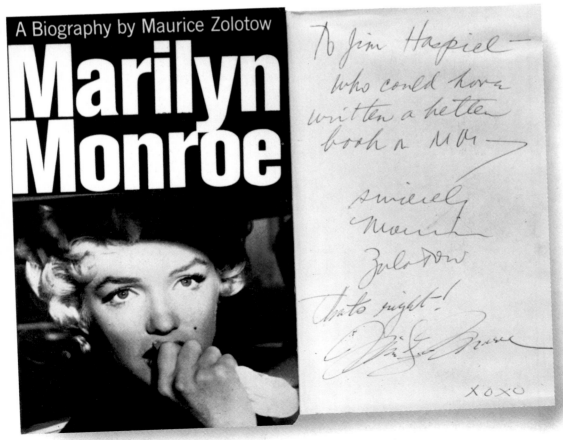

I next saw Marilyn at the Polyclinic Hospital on West 50th Street, that July 11th. She had gone there for an operation to remove her gall bladder. On her departure, she was brought outside in a wheelchair, and at the sight of Monroe, the media people and the crowd of citizens that

Maurice Zolotow wrote the first full-length biography of Marilyn, but I had to point out to him many inaccuracies. Zolotow recognized my authority to write a book, a view endorsed enthusiastically here by Marilyn herself.

This was the last picture taken of me and Marilyn together, photographed on the evening of June 14th, 1961 by Six member, Frieda Hull. Marilyn's dog, Maf, looking up at me, was a gift from Frank Sinatra.

had gathered outside the hospital had become so frenzied that the wheel-chair somehow disap-peared right out from under Marilyn! According to the next day's news-papers, it was never found, which must make it one of the oddest Monroe souv-enir items ever. At the hos-pital, I soon found myself unexpectedly entwined in several television camera cables, and I became so outraged at what was suddenly happening to me, the all-out rioting all about me, that I quite literally began to disengage the plugs on the cable wires entrapping me, thus eliminating one-by-one those images of Monroe that were being transmitted to local television stations. The hysterical crowd clearly outnumbered me both physically and psychologically; times like these, so common in Marilyn's life, caused me genuine emotional pain as regards to the safety of my Marilyn.

What 8-mm colour movie footage I was able to capture that afternoon shows a Monroe in very real distress, pain on her face, that pain only replaced by a smile when she spotted me, for in her gut she knew well by now that I would always be among her most avid protectors. Now it was okay, she was safely inside the ambulette vehicle that would carry her home to East 57th Street, waving back at me and smiling her lovely smile as the auto took its leave of the still riot-like area.

Sometime during this period, Monroe moved back to California, while still holding on to her apartment in New York City. Something had happened in 1961 that was later to be called by the individuals closest to Monroe 'the Sardi's incident'. Paula Strasberg,

Marilyn's like-family personal friend and acting coach told me this sad story, advising me that the only people who knew anything about this event were Marilyn, Marilyn's psychiatrist, Paula and her husband Lee. And, of course, the individual who instigated the situation itself, an actress Paula identified to me as she unfolded the tale. Allow me to state here that it has never made any sense to me as to why it was referred to as 'the Sardi's incident', because the happening itself actually took place inside another restaurant, Jim Downey's establishment on Eighth Avenue.

What happened, according to Paula's version via Marilyn, was that the actress in question had requested Monroe's help with 'a scene that I am preparing to do at the Actors Studio', and Monroe accepted the woman's invitation to lunch, in order 'to go over the scene with me to see if you maybe can help me out with what should be my motivation here, my inner feelings, Marilyn?' Now seated in a booth at the restaurant, the woman first plied Monroe with drinks, then gently led her into the lines of the scripted scene, which turned out to be a kind of a love scene. Sitting right there in Downey's, at a certain point in the script, the actress suddenly embraced Monroe in an obvious male-to-female way, then kissed Monroe directly and passionately on the lips!

The actress had arranged, for what exact reason nobody really knew, for a couple of people from the Press to be seated quietly across the way, to observe her in the midst of what clearly appeared to them, at that distance, to be a lesbian embrace with Marilyn Monroe, in a public place! As the woman's lips now impacted so unexpectedly upon her own mouth, the woman's tongue attempting to enter her, Monroe, realizing immediately that something was

Marilyn at an airport on February 21st, 1962 (my 24th birthday), with hairstylist, George Masters, behind her.

Opposite: Arriving at the Golden Globe Award Ceremonies in Hollywood on March 5th, 1962.

With host Steve Allen looking on, Marilyn accepts her Golden Globe Award as the 'World's Favourite Female Star'.

terribly wrong here, at once rose from the table and rushed away from the restaurant and from her actress friend. It was later that Monroe learned about 'the witnesses' who were seated nearby.

Monroe was so utterly dismayed by this incredible event that she opted never to return to any classes at the Actors Studio in New York City, a place where the actress in question was certain to be. Equally upset about the incident, Paula, too, in a show of support for Marilyn, decided to henceforth avoid the woman: 'I never went back into the Actors Studio after that, Jim,' she told me. I think that Marilyn herself then felt a total breakdown in her ability to trust many of those around her, the actress in question having been one of her friends at the Actors Studio. She couldn't understand from any angle why this had happened, couldn't understand why it had been done to her, in particular? Finally, the incident became Monroe's real and ultimate motivation for departing New York City, for moving herself back to California, to an atmosphere that suddenly loomed as something of a safety zone to her. It was the eve of 1962.

Decades later, as fate would have it, in the 1980s, I was visiting my sons' godmother, Shelley Winters, in Beverly Hills, California. I had been on the West Coast for five weeks or so, and I was about to fly home to New York City. Shelley was going to drive me to the airport, but something happened at the last minute, and she wasn't able to do it; so Shelley offered, 'I'll call a friend of mine to take you to the airport, Jim.' I said, 'Fine, Shelley,' and carried on with my preparations to leave. Soon the doorbell rang, the friend arrived, and amazingly, she turned out to be the woman of 'the Sardi's incident'! Feeling

Opposite: Marilyn holds her Award as Rock Hudson congratulates her.

very strongly the awkwardness of the situation at hand, I had more than a momentary dilemma about the ride I was about to take; after all, I loved Marilyn dearly, and this woman was known to me as one of Monroe's enemies. Shelley herself had absolutely no knowledge of what had taken place some two decades earlier, and I wasn't about to broach the subject here and now! Following introductions, Shelley and I fondly kissed goodbye, and I got into the woman's car, now sitting beside the actress of Marilyn's nightmare in the front seat, and we drove off in the direction of the airport.

En route, without my being obvious about it at all, I insinuated Marilyn's name into the conversation, at which point, the woman remarked, 'Oh, Marilyn and I worked on a scene together once, Jim; a scene I had to do at the Actors Studio.' Listening, I did not allow any extraordinary reaction to show on my face; I just wanted her to talk on, to see what she might say. The actress then told me about how she had rehearsed the scene with Marilyn, and as she went on, I was thinking to myself, 'I know something about this that you're telling me which you don't know that I know,' thinking on, 'and nobody has ever understood why you did what you did to Marilyn.' At last, we arrived at the airport, we said polite so-longs, and the actress drove off, never knowing until now (are you reading this, I hope?) of my personal knowledge of the event that took place inside Jim Downey's Restaurant so long ago, contributing so effectively to the onset of the California period that would end with the death of Marilyn Monroe.

It was the end of one decade, the beginning of another. It would soon be ten years since I'd first glimpsed Marilyn on the silver screen in *Clash by Night*. As in the beginning, we were once again separated by thousands of miles. I wrote her. In my letter, I mentioned that one of the Six, Gloria Milone, had followed her move to the West Coast. I gently apologized for my 'antics', for the excitement I so readily exhibited in her presence: 'Over the years, Marilyn, there must've been many times when I looked to you to be little more than a gaping kid.' I signed off with, 'Much love, Jimmy.'

The beige envelope was familiar. The postmark read February 8th, 1962, 7 p.m. It was addressed: 'Mr James Haspiel, 3 West 73rd Street, New York 23, New York.' The return address read: '882 North Doheny Drive, Los Angeles 46, California.' Above it were the familiar embossed letters: 'MARILYN MONROE'. And inside, on familiar beige stationery —

> *Dear Jimmy,*
> *Thanks for your nice letter; I loved hearing from you. No, I haven't seen Gloria. Now, Jimmy, how could I ever mistake you for a 'gaping kid'? Missed seeing you but will see you around New York.*
>
> *Love and kisses,*
> *Marilyn*

I received Marilyn's letter eleven days after she wrote it, on February 19th, 1962. (On that date a new life entered the universe; it was on that very day that the 'Jimmy' to whom this book is dedicated was born to Linda and James Smith.)

I read Marilyn's letter again; this time it was from her personally, this time it *was* for me.

Then came the now immortal night of May 19th, when Monroe sang 'Happy Birth-day' to President John F. Kennedy at the old Madison Square Garden, then still located at Eighth Avenue and 50th Street. I attended that event, and as a witness to the evening, I must tell you that when you now see the documentary film footage of her there, if you see the extended version, you watch as Peter

The famous birthday tribute to President Kennedy at Madison Square Garden, where Marilyn sang a breathy *Happy Birthday* to him on May 19th, 1962.

Opposite: On the set of *Something's Got to Give* in April 1962, this was the last film Marilyn worked on. The studio fired her before its completion and it was never released. Extensive unedited footage survives, which provides the clearest evidence of her undiminished acting talent and eternal beauty.

The final image captured of the star as she passes through the gates of Twentieth Century-Fox for the last time on June 1st, 1962.

Lawford introduces Monroe several times over. Well, in reality, that night of entertainment at which half of show business must have performed, was four or five hours long, and Lawford's bit was done intentionally; he introduced Monroe at various points all through the evening, each of these introductions spoken to wild applause, but to no Monroe. She didn't appear earlier because she wasn't supposed to appear. Marilyn was intended to be the grand finale of the evening, to arrive along with JFK's birthday cake. The earlier intros really were a tease for the audience, and then, during the finale, Lawford introduced her with the words: 'Mr President, the late Marilyn Monroe.' At the time, it was meant to be humorous. So finally, there she was, and I looked hard towards the stage as she sang sensually to the President, all shimmering and wonderful, the audience all but out of their minds at the very sight of her, their 'Marilyn Monroe', the persona of Norma Jeane virtually invisible now! Yes, there *she* was, there *he* was, and for those few intimates in the know, what a really spectacular 'couple' they made.

Paula Strasberg later told me that there existed personal letters written by John F. Kennedy to Marilyn, that Paula and Lee had placed 'into a safe deposit box, not to be opened for fifty years, Jim; too many people would be hurt if they were seen.' One simply cannot know the absolute truth about this, but Paula most certainly did say this to me. And when I asked Paula about Marilyn and John, asking her specifically about Robert Kennedy's role in the already rumoured triangle, Paula removed all thoughts of a romance between Marilyn and Bobby with a simple line. In 1964, to my direct question as to exactly who had been making love to whom, Paula responded, 'They're both dead, now, Jim,' quickly eliminating the still-living Bobby from the more intimate scenario.

About the night of May 19th–20th, 1962, over the years there have been many claims as to exactly where Monroe spent that evening, following her appearance at Madison Square Garden, in particular that she had slept with President Kennedy at the Carlyle Hotel. I can tell you with *authority*, that I was with Marilyn at her apartment at

On her thirty-sixth birthday, June 1st, 1962, Marilyn made her last public appearance – at a benefit baseball game.

ten minutes to four in the morning. Categorically, Marilyn was not asleep at the Carlyle Hotel, and I didn't notice the President anywhere nearby us, either! The night of entertainment at Madison Square Garden probably got underway at around eight o'clock in the evening, and must have ended sometime after midnight, after which there was a party for Kennedy and certain of the performers from the Garden that Marilyn then attended on the arm of 'my father-in-law, Isadore Miller . . .' Allowing time for her socializing at the party, then getting Isadore back to his home in Brooklyn, Marilyn's return home at nearly 4 a.m. was not unreasonable. Suffice it to say, she was in my company at ten minutes to four. I know for sure what I saw, I certainly know where I was, I know for certain where *she* was.

I looked at Marilyn, not knowing that this would be our last time together. Now she wasn't on a stage, she was here just an arm's length away from me, and I could touch her. Her face was incredibly beautiful, movingly vulnerable. Her hair looked like white spun gold. My eyes descended to the rhinestone-like gems sewn onto her dazzling gown, now eliciting flickers of light, those beams bouncing off the flesh-toned material encasing her magnificent body. Her high heels were lying beside her; Marilyn was barefoot. There was a hesitation; utterly fatigued, she was visibly upset, then she spoke. 'Oh, Jimmy . . .' The next moment remains ours alone forever. I choose to offer no explanation as to why it then happened, but I will tell you that I was destined never to forget the very last words Norma Jeane heard come forth from my tongue; in an unfortunate moment, it was with considerable anger that Marilyn's 'Jimmy' looked at her and, upon departure, muttered aloud, '*Oh, go to hell, Marilyn!*'

Sunday, August 5th, 1962. The telephone rang at eight o'clock in the morning, waking me up. 'Hello?' Frieda Hull, her voice trembling, inquired, 'Did you hear about Mazzie, Jimmy?' Quickly giving way to tears, Frieda couldn't continue. My stomach turned; never had I felt more vulnerable. The obvious was surely impossible! Immediately, I put the radio on, and without a pause, heard: 'Marilyn Monroe is dead . . .'

The following weeks were a veritable nightmare of tears born of so many vivid memories of Marilyn. My final comment to her took a grip and now haunted me, terribly so. There could be no doubt that I loved Marilyn with all my heart. Now I had to trust that she had still known that despite my outrage with her that morning of May 20th. How could she not know it? It had been eight wonderful years of adoration, of laughter, sometimes of controversy and pain; in all, the quintessential things that life and relationships are made up of. I couldn't know then that she had saved my letters and cards written to her over the years, items discovered among her personal papers a quarter of a century later. I couldn't know then about something else that was found near her lifeless body the night she died, something that was ultimately destined to redefine the nature of our friendship entirely in later years. I will tell you what it was in a moment.

Why was she gone? How had it really happened? 'Probably suicide' was the original answer served up by the officials in charge of explaining her demise. *Bullshit! Rashomon* was a 1951 film out of Japan, directed by Akira Kurosawa. An international success, in America the film won the Academy Award for Best Foreign Film. The film's plot: a group of people involved in a death present different accounts of how the murder took place. May I now present the plot of the not-necessarily imaginary scenario of my friend's last hours . . .

The President,
The Politician,
The Actor and
The Actress in
Rasho-Monroe

Fade-in . .

It was still early evening on a warm Saturday in August in the movie capital of the world.

The dining-room,
living-room, and entryway
of Marilyn's California
home. Her subscription
issue of *The New York
Times* lies on the welcome
bench.

The actress's housekeeper was napping at the other end of the L-shaped domicile. The actress was in her own bedroom, now being badgered to 'Leave my brother alone! This is getting out of hand, it's becoming too dangerous; you could devastate his political career if you don't stop seeing him now! *Right now!*' Suddenly silent, the politician gritted his teeth and clenched his fists in all-out anger. Now, his brother-in-law, the actor, also her friend, spoke up, advising the actress, 'I think you'd better listen to him, sweetie, he means what he's saying!' She could hear them both, alright, but her heart couldn't. The actress was in love with the President.

As the next minutes passed, once again voices rose, tempers flared, and suddenly the actress found herself on the floor of the bedroom, her body hurting from the bruise now welling up on her skin. At once, the two men lifted the actress up and placed her onto the bed. She was sobbing uncontrollably. Suddenly, without thinking further, the politician grabbed for a

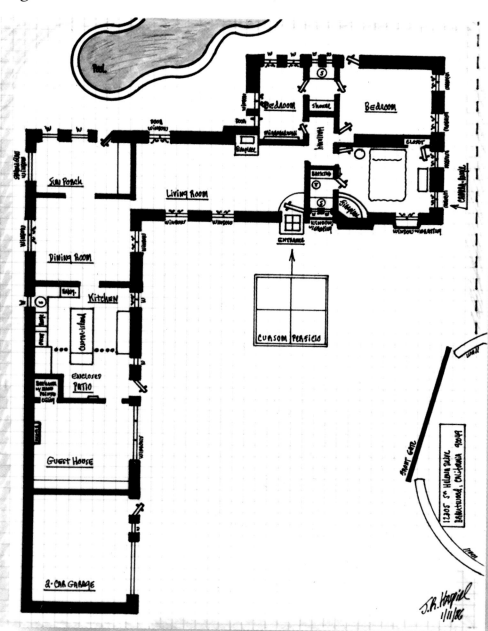

A precise floor-plan of Marilyn's final home, which I detailed in the 1980s while on a visit to LA.

pillow across the bed, placed it over her tear-stained face, and pressing down hard, he ordered the actor, 'You hold her legs down!' The struggle was brief; she fought to no avail, soon falling into an unconscious state. The room was immediately quiet. Tossing the pillow aside, the politician looked down at the actress's stilled form. The actor was now down on his knees at the foot of the bed, sobbing and muttering, his own heart racing wildly at the stark reality of the shocking thing that had just taken place so very unexpectedly. The politician's voice broke in: 'I'm getting out of here now, I have to! You stay and clean up! See if you can make it look like a suicide; I'll call you in a while!'

The actor gathered himself together and began, nervously, the awful process of resetting the scene at hand to read as a suicide. But how? The answer came fast and simple. The actress already had a known reputation among her friends for consuming large quantities of sleeping pills, and sleeping pills, if fatal, actually suffocate their victim. In fact, they are likely to produce the same autopsy results as any other form of death by suffocation. The results parallel one another.

Quickly, the actor gathered the bottles of sleeping pills from her private bathroom just off the bedroom, and he emptied them out into his pockets, then set the empty vials down on the small end table next to the bed on which she lay. Then it was time to arrange her body on the bed. As the world's greatest sex symbol, surely it would be fitting if she was

Within hours of the news of Marilyn's death, this movie house in New York City put up a marquee advertising two of her films.

discovered nude, so he peeled back the white terry-cloth bathrobe, pulling it all the way off of her. Now the actor couldn't stop himself from staring at her, this lady of the President's fantasies, and then, without any warning at all, it happened; she moved! The actress wasn't dead – *not yet*!

Realizing an opportunity to reverse the direction of all that had happened here in this room tonight, the actor reached for the actress's bedside telephone, and hurriedly called for an ambulance. The next minutes seemed to him an eternity, but soon they were rushing the actress towards the hospital, rushing her towards help. But finally, it *was* too late; the actress expired in the ambulance, en route to the hospital. The actor, an individual with a powerful connection by marriage to the highest office in the land, now ordered the driver to 'Pull the ambulance over, I have to think!' What to do? 'Turn the ambulance around, we're going back to the house . . .'

Back at the house, the actor now proceeded to reinstate the original plan to stage a suicide scene. With her nude form placed belly-down on the bed, her legs now somewhat akimbo (the actor didn't realize that death by suffocation causes the body to invert itself into the fetal position), he now drew the bedsheet up towards her shoulders. He then placed the telephone receiver in her hand, and taking her other hand, placed a stiffening finger into the dial on the front of her telephone. Standing back, the actor checked the scene again. Something was bothering him, the feeling nagged at him, but having done all he could think of to do, the time had arrived to take leave of the bedroom. Flipping the automatic latch-lock on the inside of the actress's bedroom door, the actor took one final look at her lifeless form there on the bed, then quietly stepped outside into the tiny hallway and drew the door shut, listening as the lock mechanism did its duty.

It was then that it suddenly struck him that he had failed to leave a glass by her bedside! After all, if the actress had just swallowed an entire bottle of sleeping pills, she must have required at least some liquid help in the process. Anxiously, he tried the doorknob, to no avail. The room was secured, with its tragic contents, to remain undisturbed for the next few hours. He thought hard. Yes, of course; she had her private bathroom in there! They would think that the actress had swallowed the pills at her bathroom sink, filling her bathroom glass as many times as needed to get the devils down, and had then made her way back to the bed to die. What the actor didn't know this time was that the plumbing in the actress's private bathroom had been shut off completely to allow repair work to be done. The bathroom, too, was bare of any of the usual items one might expect to find in there; *there was no glass*! The actress had in fact been using another bathroom in the house while her own was shut down, the bathroom that connected her two guest rooms. Hours from now the actress's bedroom door would open again to reveal what looked to all eyes to be her probable suicide.

In time, all three of these men in the actress's life, the President, his brother, the politician, and the actor would pay the price for what took place in her bedroom that warm Saturday night in August.

.... Fade-out.

The story of 'Rasho-Monroe' in its entire pathetic and convincing detail had been revealed to me halfway through the 1980s, and *before* a Marilynesque Madonna turned up on television's popular staple, *Saturday Night Live*, an outing on which the mega-star portrayed 'Marilyn Monroe' in a skit in which Kennedy smothered her to death with a pillow, before an audience of millions of viewers! I thought to myself, I know where this is really coming from (I'd been told earlier that an executive at the television network was privy to the details of 'Rasho-Monroe'), but what must the rest of the viewing audience be thinking right now? After all, they all 'know' that Marilyn Monroe did herself in with sleeping pills, so, this isn't making any sense? Welcome to reality, people.

Back in 1962, on the night Marilyn died, to the left of the bed on which her body was discovered there sat a chest-of-drawers, and in that bureau was found a plain manila

Top: Behind the curtains lies Marilyn's flower-draped casket at her funeral service on August 8th, 1962.

Centre: In October 1969, my wife Barbara and I drove up to Westwood Memorial Cemetery to visit Marilyn's crypt.

Above: My white rose rests among Joe DiMaggio's red roses on the face of Marilyn's crypt in July 1970.

It was this photograph that was found in Marilyn's bedside cabinet after her death, along with pictures of her stepchildren, Joe DiMaggio Jnr and Jane and Bobby Miller.

envelope, inside which there were some photographs of what might be called her children; in fact, these were pictures of her stepchildren. Images of Joe DiMaggio Jr, images of Jane and Bobby Miller, the children to whom Marilyn had been a stepmother during her lifetime. The only other image in that envelope was a picture of Jimmy Haspiel. 'For the one and only Jimmy, . . . Love you, Marilyn.' I'll just leave it there.

And while I will not say how this was accomplished, I can tell you that there is a snapshot of Marilyn and myself, a small message from me to her written on its back, now in the crypt with her remains.

Little more than a month after Marilyn died, on September 8th, 1962, I hosted a 'Tribute to Marilyn' night at my then home on West 73rd Street, an evening that was attended by, among others, the Monroe Six, and by Paula and Lee Strasberg. I showed those gathered together there my home movies of Marilyn, we all looked over the hundreds of candid snapshots that we had taken of her over the years, and we reminisced long into the night about our 'Mazzie'. Throughout the evening, Lee remained totally silent, conspicuously so, and I was quietly dismayed by this. But later on, as the Strasbergs departed, at the door, Lee said to me about the evening now ending, 'A lot of love went into that, Jim.' What neither of us knew in that moment was that these decades later the love is yet there, firmly, securely in place, eternal.

'I remember when you were seventeen, Jimmy.' Well, dear Marilyn, I still remember that first night at the St Regis, when you were twenty-eight, and for much of the world, you always will be that age, ever beautiful, ever wistful, ever the beacon of light so wonderfully realized out of the quiet dreams of a child known as Norma Jeane.

God bless, peace,
Jimmy.

INDEX

Page numbers in italics indicate illustrations
Abbreviations: cap =information given in caption
JH =James Haspiel
MM =Marilyn Monroe

ACKNOWLEDGEMENTS

FOR IMAGE CONTRIBUTIONS, my considerable gratitude to: Gloria Milone, Richard Rodriguez, Frieda Hull, George Rehm, and to (the late) Teri Arden, Gloria Chittick, Phil Claude, Eileen Collins, Fred Guiles, Barbara Haspiel, (the late) Walter Horoshko, Jimmy Leggi, John Reilly, Lou Valenti, and for the beautiful reproductions herein, to Phil Vance and his talented crew (Clay, Cory, Emanuel, Karen, Kevin, Reggie, Tracy) at Photovision, and with love and lust to the delightful Roberta 'Robbie' Blue.

FOR STORY CONTRIBUTIONS, appreciation must go to: (the late) Paula Strasberg, my friend Tony Summers, and to Marilyn, of course, for the wonderful eight years she so generously gave to me.

FOR PROFESSIONAL SUPPORT, I owe thanks to: Eve Arnold, Cindy Adams, Denis Ferrara, Liz Smith, my editor, Judy Martin, and especially to my dynamic publisher, a one-of-a-kind gentleman, Robert Smith.

FOR GENERAL ASSISTANCE, thank yous go to: Reha Bennicasa, Ray Goggin, and, in particular, to Manuel Guzman.

MOST IMPORTANTLY, FOR EMOTIONAL SUPPORT, I am eternally indebted to: My wife Barbara, our sons Dean and Michael, my sister Cathy, Julio Herrero and the family of my S.O., especially Josh and Linda, my (late) great friend, Bruce Martin (we did it, buddy!), and just because . . . Robert 'Bobby' Moore.

I LOVE EACH AND EVERY ONE OF YOU VERY MUCH.